# InsightOut

Also by Tina Seelig

*inGenius: A Crash Course on Creativity*

*What I Wish I Knew When I Was 20*

# InsightOut

## Get Ideas Out of Your Head and Into the World

## Tina Seelig

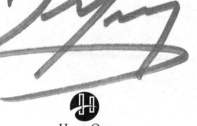

HarperOne
*An Imprint of HarperCollinsPublishers*

HarperOne

All Invention Cycle graphics are provided by Tina Seelig and are used by permission; illustration on page 41 is provided by Kevin Meier and is used by permission; illustration on page 42 is provided by Elad Segev and Odelia Kohn-Oppenheim and is used by permission; illustration on page 103 is provided by Katherine Young and is used by permission; illustration on page 117 is provided by Greg McKeweon and is used by permission; illustration on page 129 is provided by CanStockPhoto, Inc and is used by permission; illustration on page 172 is provided by Maya Eilam and is used by permission.

HarperCollins books may be purchased for educational, business, or sales promotional use. For information please e-mail the Special Markets Department at SPsales@harpercollins.com.

HarperCollins website: http://www.harpercollins.com

HarperCollins®, 🏭®, and HarperOne™ are trademarks of HarperCollins Publishers.

FIRST EDITION

*Designed by Ralph Fowler*

Library of Congress Cataloging-in-Publication Data
    Seelig, Tina Lynn.
      Insight out : get ideas out of your head and into the world / Tina Seelig. —
First edition.
      pages cm
    ISBN 978–0–06–230127–7
     1. Creative thinking. 2. Creative ability. 3. Creative ability in business.
   4. Technological innovations. 5. Entrepreneurship. I. Title.
    BF408.S3866   2015
    153.3'5—dc23     2015009853

15  16  17  18  19   RRD(H)   10  9  8  7  6  5  4  3  2  1

*For Michael, my superhero*

# Contents

# Contents

# Letter to Readers

A few years ago, I stumbled upon a letter that I had written to myself thirty years earlier. I was looking through an old box of correspondence in search of a note from a childhood friend who had reached out to me soon after my book, *What I Wish I Knew When I Was 20*, was released. While digging through the envelopes, I found a letter that I had written to myself on the eve of my twentieth birthday. Reading the words scribbled on a lined notepad flung me back in time to an era when I was filled with big dreams, and even bigger doubts about how to achieve them. The letter poignantly describes how challenging it is to harness your potential and bring your dreams to life. It was also a stunning confirmation that the book I had just released, which presented a crash course on making your place in the world, *was* what I wish I had known when I was twenty. Below is an excerpt from that letter:

> I am going to be twenty this next month, and I'm supposed to be a real person by now: an adult, responsible, having a purpose. I feel so far from that now. I want to be interesting, and I don't find myself interesting. I want to be intelligent, and I'm not. I want to be the type of person I would like to meet, and it seems so fruitless. . . . Perhaps the goals I have for myself are ridiculously high and I should stop before I start.

Reading this letter was a reminder of how far I had come—from a twenty-year-old filled with anxiety about where to begin my journey into adulthood, to an adult who has managed to navigate a circuitous path to a gratifying profession. Like countless others, when I was in my twenties I was filled with a palpable drive to do something that was meaningful, but lacked an understanding of how to tap into my wellspring of energy to find a path toward that goal. Thirty years later, I believe there are three crucial elements needed to build a bridge to the future you want to create:

The first is an entrepreneurial mind-set that allows you to see the world as opportunity-rich. It is up to you to make your own luck, to see that most rules are recommendations, and to give yourself permission to challenge assumptions. Those lessons are captured in *What I Wish I Knew When I Was 20*. As I wrote in that book:

Boundless possibilities result from extracting yourself from your comfort zone, being willing to fail, having a healthy disregard for the impossible, and seizing every opportunity to be fabulous. Yes, these actions inject chaos into your life and keep you off-balance. But they also take you places you couldn't even have imagined and provide a lens through which to see problems as opportunities. Above all, they give you growing confidence that problems can be solved.

The second is a specific set of tools for solving problems and taking advantage of opportunities that you inevitably encounter along the way. Those are described in my next book, *inGenius: A Crash Course on Creativity*, which illustrates how to harness factors both inside yourself and in the outside environment to unlock the pathway to invention:

Creativity can be enhanced by honing your ability to observe and learn, by connecting and combining ideas, by reframing problems, and by moving beyond the first right answers. You can boost your creative output by building habitats that foster problem solving, crafting environments that support the generation of new ideas, building teams that are optimized for innovation, and contributing to a culture that encourages experimentation.

And third is a clear road map for moving from inspiration to implementation. That's the book you are holding now.

I'm fortunate to have the opportunity to teach these skills to students at Stanford University. As a professor of the practice in the Department of Management Science and Engineering and executive director of the Stanford Technology Ventures Program (STVP)—the entrepreneurship center at Stanford School of Engineering—my role is to help young people identify and seize opportunities. Our goal at STVP is to foster the skills that will enable them to build their career, contribute to the organizations they join, and lead a fulfilling life. We do this in formal courses, extracurricular programs, and with workshops for students and faculty from all over the world. The essence of STVP's philosophy is captured in a slogan painted on our wall:

---

*Entrepreneurs do much more than imaginable with much less than seems possible.*

---

As this message communicates, entrepreneurship isn't just about starting companies. It's about starting anything! Entrepreneurship involves building the knowledge, skills, and attitudes needed to see problems as opportunities and to leverage resources to bring ideas to fruition. This is just as relevant to those who are starting a rock band or planning a trip around the world as it is to those who are launching a company. This book presents a framework for bringing your ideas to life—*whatever* those ideas may be.

As with my other books, I invite you into my classroom at Stanford. The words on these pages are designed to stimulate your thinking and your actions. I introduce general concepts and then offer stories to illustrate them. I also share my personal experiences, those of my students, and research related to the concepts discussed. Many of the examples come from innovators and entrepreneurs in Silicon Valley; these are complemented by cases from around the globe.

At the conclusion of each chapter, I suggest projects you can do to reinforce the concepts. These projects are an important part of the experience: they provide stepping-stones for moving from ideas to actions. Some require a few minutes of personal reflection, and others require putting down the book and taking on a specific task. I strongly believe that all learning is experiential. If you aren't actively engaged in the material, it won't stick.

I welcome feedback on how you used the book and the projects it has inspired. You can reach me at tseelig@gmail. com and follow me on Twitter @tseelig.

Creativity rules!
Tina

# InsightOut

# Introduction

## *Inspiration to Implementation*

Over 60 percent of prison inmates in California end up back in prison within three years. This recidivism rate is a proxy for a lack of hope. Those who are released from prison, often decades after they were first incarcerated, face a world with few options, piercing prejudice, and little guidance on how to rebuild their lives. Many look into their future and see nothing but fog, with no clear path ahead. No wonder so many slip back into a life of crime and return to prison.

In an attempt to address this daunting problem, successful entrepreneurs Chris Redlitz and Beverly Parenti started the Last Mile program to prepare prison inmates at San Quentin State Prison in California for successful reentry into freedom through training in business and technology. Along with other volunteers with expertise in a wide variety of fields, they meet with a group of forty prisoners twice a week for six months, teaching them about entrepreneurship and helping them develop skills, such as written communication, public speaking, and computer proficiency.

Participants create a business idea that uses technology to address a social problem, and learn how to give a five-minute pitch that effectively communicates their plan. At the end of six months, they present their idea to an audience of business leaders and fellow inmates. Past projects developed by the men include: Fitness Monkey, a startup crafted to help addicts replace drugs with a healthy addiction to fitness; TechSage, which helps ex-cons become mobile app developers so they can get a job after their incarceration; and the Funky Onion, which buys bruised fruits and vegetables cheaply and sells them to restaurants that will cook them and thus don't mind their "funky" appearance.

The most important thing these men learn is how to see themselves as entrepreneurs who can carve a path toward their future. This isn't just an issue in prison—you don't have to spend time locked up to feel rudderless. Countless people around the world don't feel confident crafting the lives they hope to lead. They don't know where they're headed or how to navigate around the obstacles in their path. They don't see themselves as innovators, responsible for and capable of inventing their own future.

.　　.　　.

It's a crime not to teach young people to be entrepreneurial. We are each responsible for building our own lives and for repairing the broader problems of the world, and the only way to do so is with the knowledge, skills, and attitudes required to bring ideas to fruition. Unfortunately, most formal education deals with memorization as opposed to innovation. It focuses on learning about heroes as opposed to teaching students to be heroic. And it presents problems with one right answer as opposed to real-life challenges with an endless number of viable solutions. People should emerge from school with *agency,* feeling empowered to address the opportunities and challenges that await them.

Many educators believe that you can't teach those skills. They see innovation and entrepreneurship as inborn traits, such as eye or hair color, that can't be changed. This is untrue—these skills can certainly be learned, and it behooves us to teach people of all ages to be entrepreneurial, enabling them to invent the world in which they want to live.

This begs the question, Why do people think that you can't teach creativity and entrepreneurship? I believe that this view stems from the lack of a clear vocabulary and a process for moving from inspiration to execution. Other fields—such as physics, biology, math, and music—have a huge advantage when it comes to teaching those topics. They have defined terms and a taxonomy of relationships that provide a structured approach for mastering needed skills. For example, if we didn't have definitions for force (F), mass (M), and acceleration (A), and a formula that describes their relationship (F = m × a), we wouldn't have cars, airplanes, or rocket ships. The definitions and equations allow us to de-scribe fundamental principles and then apply them in con-structive ways.

We've been complacent by using a loose vocabulary to de-fine the creative process. When I ask people in any setting, from a classroom to a corporate office, to define creativity, I get a range of responses. Most people start with "To me creativity is . . ." And the most common completion of this phrase is "thinking outside the box." When asked what that actually means, they don't know. This cliché is derived from the solution to the "nine dots" puzzle, where the goal is to connect nine dots, shown below, by drawing four or fewer straight lines that pass through each of the dots while never lifting the pencil from the paper.

One way to solve the puzzle is to draw lines that extend beyond the boundary of an imaginary "box" around the dots. Hence, think outside the box.

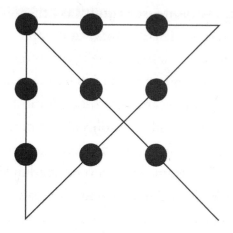

Jim Adams, in his landmark book *Conceptual Blockbusting*, describes a long list of additional solutions to this puzzle that stretch the boundaries of the imagination, including crumpling up the paper and drawing one line that intersects all the dots, having one line that circles the entire globe to intersect all the dots, or using a very fat pen that intersects all the dots in one swipe.

Since most people don't know the origin of the expression "think outside the box," they use it as a catchall and cliché phrase, which renders it meaningless. In reality, creativity requires a complex set of skills, attitudes, and actions, intimately related to imagination, innovation, and entrepreneurship. To harness our creativity, we need a robust set of definitions for all parts of the creative and entrepreneurial process. A cliché tagline is woefully insufficient.

To be honest, I've been just as guilty as others in not clearly defining the terms related to innovation and entrepreneurship. I've taught a course called Creativity and Innovation for over a dozen years, and for most of that time I used the words *imagination, creativity,* and *innovation* almost interchangeably. I taught a set of skills and tools for reframing problems, challenging assumptions, and connecting ideas; however, I didn't have a larger framework into which they fit.

After years immersed in this field, I've realized that this is a huge missing piece. Without a robust framework, we can't teach or learn the skills needed to consistently move through the creative process. My goal in this book is to bring together what we know about creativity with what we know about entrepreneurship so that we can define, learn, teach, and practice these skills in a rigorous and reproducible manner. Innovation and entrepreneurship are powerful instruments for individuals, teams, organizations, and entire communities. With these tools we gain personal empowerment, foster organizational change, and become prepared to address pressing problems that face the world.

To begin, there is a hierarchy of skills, starting with imagination:

*Imagination leads to creativity.*
*Creativity leads to innovation.*
*Innovation leads to entrepreneurship.*

This scaffolding of skills can be compared to those involved with reading and writing: Babies naturally babble, making *noises* to communicate. They learn how to harness those noises and combine them to form *words*. They then learn to connect words to compose *sentences*, and then combine those sentences to craft *stories*. Those stories influence all those who hear them. Educators take great care to teach all the foundational skills along the way, including vocabulary, grammar, reading, and writing.

Noise ➡ Word ➡ Sentence ➡ Story

We are in desperate need of a complementary methodology for learning how to unlock creativity, innovation, and entrepreneurship. Below are proposed definitions and relationships for moving from imagination to entrepreneurship. I call this the *Invention Cycle*. The cycle encapsulates the entire process and illustrates how the end leads back to the beginning. It also provides a shortcut so that we don't have to list all the steps each time we refer to the progression of going from ideas to actions.

### The Invention Cycle

- *Imagination* is envisioning things that do not exist.

- *Creativity* is *applying* imagination to address a challenge.

- *Innovation* is *applying* creativity to generate unique solutions.

- *Entrepreneurship* is *applying* innovation, to bring unique ideas to fruition, inspiring others' imagination.

Let's look at each of these stages in turn:

*Imagination is envisioning things that do not exist.* This requires curiosity, engagement, and the ability to conceive of ideas in your mind. This natural skill is influenced by your experiences, both real and fictional. Therefore, the more diverse your inputs, including travel, books, cuisines, music, and films, the more robust your imagination. Your imaginative ideas can live quite comfortably in your mind, or you can share them with others. For example, I might imagine an animal that is a cross between a cat and a bird, or a menu where dessert is served first. I can keep these thoughts to myself, or share them as I did above.

*Creativity is* applying *imagination to address a challenge.* Creative ideas fill a specific need *and* are manifest in the world. They are new ideas to *you,* but not necessarily new to others. It is important to distinguish between imagination and creativity. It's imaginative to fill your thoughts with scenes of the seashore, and it's creative to apply your imagination to paint a picture of the scene. It's imaginative to envision a solar car, and creative to actually build one.

This usage is consistent with scholarly work on creativity. Mark Runco and Garrett Jaeger of the Torrance Creativity Center at the University of Georgia, reviewed the range of scholarly definitions for creativity in a *Creativity Research Journal* article titled "The Standard Definition of Creativity." In summary, they write, "Creativity requires both originality and effectiveness. . . . Originality is vital for creativity but is not sufficient. . . . Original things must be effective to be creative." Echoing this, Sir Ken Robinson, an expert in this field, notes that "creative ideas don't have to be original to the whole world, but they must be original to you, and they must have value."

*Innovation is* applying *creativity to generate unique solutions.* In contrast to creativity, innovative ideas are new to the world, not just new to the inventor. This necessitates looking at the world with a fresh perspective, and involves challenging assumptions, reframing situations, and connecting ideas from disparate disciplines. The resulting breakthrough ideas reveal opportunities and tackle challenges that haven't been addressed the same way before. On the surface, this might seem subtly different from creativity. On the contrary, it is critically important, since innovation requires pushing far past everyday creative problem solving.

Companies pursue innovation because they want breakthrough ideas to compete in a highly dynamic marketplace. Examples of innovations abound in today's world, including 3D printing (1984), the web browser (1990), and insulation made from fungus (2007). Innovations occur in all disciplines and endeavors, including math, art, music, and cooking.

*Entrepreneurship* is *applying* innovation, to bring unique ideas to fruition, thereby inspiring others' imagination. Clearly, entrepreneurship is needed in businesses that are designed to commercialize innovations, but it is equally important in all endeavors that depend upon entrepreneurial thinking to address thorny problems. Entrepreneurial doctors develop and deliver lifesaving procedures; entrepreneurial educators invent and deploy effective teaching techniques; and entrepreneurial policymakers craft and implement groundbreaking laws to address social problems.

## Introduction

Mistakenly, many people conflate the words *innovation* and *entrepreneurship* by stating that innovations *need* to have a significant impact on the world. This is terribly confusing. There are plenty of innovations—breakthrough ideas—that never make it out of the garage or laboratory for a variety of reasons. Perhaps there isn't a drive to commercialize a particular innovation; maybe there are financial hurdles or cultural barriers to implementation. But even if an innovation doesn't reach escape velocity, it is still an innovation.

The Invention Cycle is a virtuous cycle: entrepreneurs manifest their ideas by inspiring others' imagination. This includes those who join the effort, fund the venture, and purchase the products. This model is relevant to startups and established firms, as well as innovators of all types where the realization of a new idea—whether a product, service, or work of art—results in a collective increase in imagination. Consider how platforms such as the iPhone, crayons, and even the kitchen stove have unleashed the imagination and creativity of millions of people who have been inspired by the possibilities they unlock; and how leaders of any organization, from a football team to a research team, can inspire the imagination of compatriots. An entrepreneurial spirit infects others, leading to wave upon wave of imagination, creativity, innovation, and entrepreneurship.

The Invention Cycle framework also allows us to parse the pathway, describing the actions and attitudes that are required to teach and learn these skills. We can look at each stage and determine how to master its skills before moving on to the next stage.

I have distilled each stage of the cycle into one representative action and one representative attitude that need to happen at that particular stage:

### Attitudes and Actions of the Invention Cycle

- Imagination requires *engagement* and the ability to *envision* alternatives.

- Creativity requires *motivation* and *experimentation* to address a challenge.

- Innovation requires *focusing* and *reframing* to generate unique solutions.

- Entrepreneurship requires *persistence* and the ability to *inspire* others.

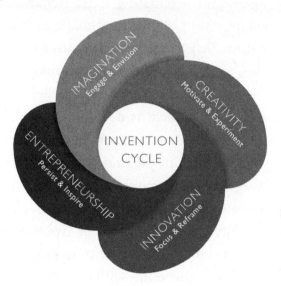

Let's look at an example to see these principles at work: As a Biodesign Innovation Fellow at Stanford University, Kate Rosenbluth spent months in the hospital shadowing neurologists and neurosurgeons. Along with her teammates with backgrounds in medicine, engineering, and business, their goal was to find the biggest unmet needs of physicians and their patients.

In the imagination stage, which required engagement and envisioning, Kate and her team made lists of hundreds of problems that needed solving, from outpatient issues to surgical challenges. By being immersed in the hospital and cultivating a watchful eye, they were able to see countless opportunities for improvement that had been overlooked.

During this process, the team was struck by how many people struggle with debilitating hand tremors that keep them from doing daily tasks, such as holding a coffee cup or buttoning a shirt. They learned that as many as eight million people in the United States experience neurological diseases that cause tremors, and experience little relief from drugs. The most effective treatment is deep brain stimulation, an onerous and expensive intervention that requires permanently implanting wires in the brain and a battery pack in the chest wall. By being actively engaged, the team envisioned the possibility of an alternate solution.

In the creativity stage, powered by motivation and experimentation, the team dove into the process of looking for potential solutions by meeting with experts, combing the literature, and testing alternative treatments. They began experimenting with new treatments and reinvented some solutions that had been tried before.

In the innovation stage, Kate and her team had an insight that changed the way that they thought about treating tremors. They were intrigued that while patients were focused on the symptoms in their arms and hands, the existing therapies focused mostly on the brain. This insight led to the development of wearable devices that treat tremors at the source. Not only is it effective, but it works without the side effects of medications or the risks of brain surgery.

In the entrepreneurship stage, Kate launched a company, Cala Health, to develop and deliver effective, safe and affordable medical devices for treating neurological diseases. There would be innumerable challenges along the way to bringing the products to market, including hiring a team, getting FDA approval, raising subsequent rounds of funding, and manufacturing and marketing the device. These tasks would require persistence and inspiring others to fund the venture, join the firm, and buy the product. While developing the first product, Kate had additional insights, stimulating new ideas for treating other diseases with a similar approach, coming full circle to imagination!

It is crucial to point out that once you go through the Invention Cycle several times, you start to use all of the skills in concert. The framework provides a guide for mastering the skills needed to manifest ideas, providing scaffolding that strengthens with use. Also, not every person in an entrepreneurial endeavor needs to have every skill in the cycle. However, every venture needs to cover every base. Without imaginers who engage with the world and envision alternatives, there won't be compelling opportunities to address. Without creators who are motivated to address a challenge and to experiment to find a solution, routine problems won't get solved. Without innovators who focus on challenging assumptions and reframing problems, there won't be fresh ideas. And without entrepreneurs who are persistent and inspire others, innovations will sit on the shelf.

In addition, entrepreneurs of all types can implement *creative* ideas, as opposed to innovative ideas. This is what happens when someone opens a new coffee shop or starts a cover band. They are short-circuiting the Invention Cycle by applying their imagination to address a challenge (creativity), but not applying their creativity to come up with a unique solution (innovation.) There isn't a problem with this. They miss the chance, however, to push further, coming up with ways to make their venture or adventure distinct.

The Invention Cycle model underpins related frameworks for innovation and entrepreneurship, such as design thinking and the lean startup methodology. Both of these frameworks focus on how individuals, teams, and organizations define problems, generate solutions, build prototypes, and iterate on the ideas based on feedback on their way to developing successful solutions. Just as we must master arithmetic before we dive into algebra or calculus, we need to develop an entrepreneurial mind-set and methodology before we tackle problems in our everyday lives, design products, or launch ventures. In the final chapter, I provide a more detailed description of how the Invention Cycle builds upon each of these models.

In the coming chapters we will dissect the Invention Cycle and then reassemble it. Each part of the book—Imagination, Creativity, Innovation, and Entrepreneurship—has an opening story that sets the stage for the following two chapters; and each chapter includes projects that allow you to practice the described skills.

The first section of the book focuses on how to enhance your imagination by engaging in the world around you and visualizing something new and different. The key takeaway is that you need to begin with curiosity, which opens doors to countless opportunities to identify challenges that need to be addressed, and then envision alternatives.

The second section discusses how to apply your imagination to generate creative ideas. It illustrates the importance of motivation and commitment in tackling a challenge, and the role of performing experiments to test your solutions. Motivation and experimentation are closely linked, since motivation naturally leads to experimentation, and the results then refuel your motivation.

The third section shows how to apply your creativity to generate innovative solutions. This process requires you to focus your attention and to reframe the way you look at a particular situation. This necessitates the ability to push through emotional, intellectual, and social blocks and actively approach the opportunity from different perspectives.

The fourth section shows how to apply innovations, implementing ideas and inspiring others. This last step encompasses all the prior actions and attitudes, as well as dogged persistence and the ability to bring others along with you.

With clear definitions for imagination, creativity, innovation, and entrepreneurship, and a taxonomy that illustrates their relationships, the Invention Cycle defines the pathway from inspiration to implementation. The framework captures the attitudes and actions that are necessary to foster innovation and to bring breakthrough ideas to the world. By understanding the Invention Cycle and honing the necessary attitudes and actions, you can identify more opportunities, challenge more assumptions, generate unique solutions, and bring more ideas to fruition. These powerful tools will help you chart a path toward the life you want to lead.

## Project

Write a letter to yourself describing what you hope to achieve in the future. Select the time frame that makes the most sense to you, and be as specific as you like. The goal of this exercise is to get you into the mind-set of thinking about charting a path toward your objectives. There will be opportunities to revisit the letter in chapter 2 and again at the end, so please consider it a first draft that will be revised.

# Part One

# Imagination

## *Engage and Envision*

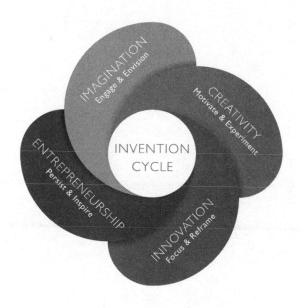

Scott Harrison's life was a mess. After ten years of working as a nightclub promoter where his goal was to entice others to go to clubs and get as drunk as possible, he was completely miserable and surrounded by what he calls a "trail of wreckage." In a lecture at Stanford he said,

. . . by the age of 28 I have assumed every single vice that you would imagine comes with nightlife. I smoke 2.5 packs of Marlboro a day. I drink excessively. I am a coke user, an MDMA user, an X user. I have a gambling problem, a pornography problem and a strip club problem. So thankfully I woke up out of my stupor after 10 years of this. I was in Punta del Este in South America . . . and it just dawned on me that I am not only the most miserable person I know, I'm the worst person I know. I mean there is no one more selfish and sycophantic than I was. And I realized that the legacy I was creating, what I was going to be known for, was that guy who threw parties and just got people wasted. And there was kind of wreckage everywhere.

In a state of disgust about what his life had become, Scott made the decision that he needed to change everything. He asked himself, "What would the opposite of my life look like?" After weeks of reflection, his answer was to offer his services to a humanitarian organization so that he could help those in need.

Scott reached out to a long list of social service groups, volunteering to help. They all turned him down. He clearly didn't look like someone who was capable of contributing. Undeterred, he continued his quest and was finally accepted as a volunteer by Mercy Ships, an organization that sends floating hospitals to the poorest regions of the world to provide free medical care. They told Scott that he could participate if he paid his own way. He jumped at the chance.

Doctors on Mercy Ships volunteer their time for two weeks, doing surgery and supplying medication to those in need. The ship that Scott boarded headed to Liberia, in West Africa. His job was to serve as the photojournalist, capturing the stories of those who received care from the medical staff. The experience opened Scott's eyes to a world of suffering. There were thousands of people with devastating illnesses, many of which were caused by water contaminated by bacteria, parasites, and sewage. His photos showed young and old people whose lives had been destroyed by the lack of clean drinking water. He decided that he needed to do something to contribute to a solution.

Upon returning to New York City in 2006, Scott founded charity:water with the goal of providing safe drinking water to the eight hundred million people on the planet who don't have it. Building on his skills as a club promoter, he rallied support from millions of people around the world, including leaders of high-profile companies who have, in turn, used their influence to reach even more people. Charity:water's tactics are straightforward—they dig wells to reach fresh water, build rain catchment systems, and install sand filters, partnering with local groups to determine appropriate locations.

There are two relevant lessons from Scott Harrison's story. First, passion follows engagement. You can best envision what you hope to accomplish after experiences that pique your imagination. As with Scott, before it's your calling, it's something you probably know nothing about. Second, we each decide the stage on which we will play out our lives. There are a myriad of options, and it is up to each of us to make that choice.

Making things happen begins by imagining what you hope to accomplish. In this section, we'll explore this first stage of the Invention Cycle, showing how engaging and envisioning allow you to define the future you want to create.

Chapter 1

# Engage

## *The Keys to the Building*

Imagine staring at one painting for three hours. That's what Jennifer Roberts, professor of History of Art and Architecture at Harvard, asks her students to do. This is part of a larger assignment in which the students intensively study one work of art. Before diving into secondary research in books or journals, they need to spend a painfully long time just observing the piece. At first, the students rebel, complaining that there can't possibly be that much to see in a single object. When they're done, however, they admit that they were "astonished by the potential this process unlocked."

Jennifer Roberts shares her own experience with a 1765 painting by John Singleton Copley, called *A Boy with a*

*Flying Squirrel,* in this excerpt from an article about her observations:

> It took me nine minutes to notice that the shape of the boy's ear precisely echoes that of the ruff along the squirrel's belly—and that Copley was making some kind of connection between the animal and the human body and the sensory capacities of each. It was 21 minutes before I registered the fact that the fingers holding the chain exactly span the diameter of the water glass beneath them. It took a good 45 minutes before I realized that the seemingly random folds and wrinkles in the background curtain are actually perfect copies of the shapes of the boy's ear and eye, as if Copley had imagined those sensory organs distributing or imprinting themselves on the surface behind him.

This exercise demonstrates that looking at something briefly doesn't necessarily mean really *seeing* it. This is the case with all our senses. We so often listen but don't really hear, touch without really feeling, look without really seeing.

To illustrate this point, I assigned a similar project to students in one of my courses. They were asked to take a silent walk for an hour, and to capture all that they heard and saw. Some chose a city setting, others the woods, and some sat at their own kitchen table. They made long lists of observations, realizing in the process that on most days they move so quickly—and noisily—through their lives that they miss the chance to observe what's happening around them. This type of observation is not just a nice-to-have addition to our lives, but is the key to a door of opportunities. By actively engaging in the world, you begin noticing patterns and opportunities.

Consider the story of the founding of Lyft, which along with other ride-sharing firms is changing the way people get around town. It all started in Zimbabwe, Africa, where Logan Green was traveling for pleasure. He noticed that drivers traveling on the crowded streets picked up people along the way. A small car might be packed with ten people, all happy to hitch a ride. Logan contrasted this with his experience back at home in the United States, where most cars have a single passenger and the roads are clogged with commuters. He was inspired to consider a similar concept at home. This was the birth of Zimride, named for Zimbabwe.

Over time the strategy for Zimride evolved from arranging carpools for universities and companies to a mobile ride-sharing platform. The company changed its name to Lyft, but the initial vision for the firm remained, triggered by Logan's observation of ride sharing along a bustling road in Africa.

I often meet individuals who are desperately looking deep inside themselves to find something that will drive their passion. They miss the fact that, for most of us, our actions *lead to* our passion, not the other way around. Passions are not innate, but grow from our experiences. For example, if you never heard a violin, kicked a ball, or cracked an egg, you'd never know that you enjoy classical music, soccer, or cooking, respectively.

Consider Scott Harrison's story, told in the opening to part 1. He applied to volunteer at dozens of organizations and joined the one group that accepted him. It could have been *any* organization. In fact, it didn't matter which one. Once he was involved, he started experiencing things he'd never seen before, and started asking questions—lots of questions. He wanted to know why there were so many sick people in Liberia, why they had illnesses he had never seen before, and what was causing those diseases. The answers to these questions moved him to ask even more questions about how to address the problem of waterborne illnesses. Before he got involved, he didn't have a passion to deliver clean water to millions of people. His passion grew from engagement.

Your first step toward developing a passion need not be glamorous. If you took a job as a waiter in a restaurant, for instance, you would have the chance to interact with hundreds of people each day and to see the world from a unique perspective. There are countless lessons you would learn from this experience, along with opportunities for inspiration. For example, you might discover secrets to effective customer service and then dive into learning how to help others improve their hospitality skills. You might become fascinated with the dietary requirements of some of your customers and then decide to open a restaurant that addresses their needs. Or you might talk with a customer and discover that she has diabetes and, after learning about her challenges, take on that cause.

Just as there are almost infinite passions you could develop, so too are there wide-ranging directions you could take your new passion once it grips you. If you decide to focus on customer service, for example, you might develop a guide for best practices in the hospitality industry, launch a consulting business, make a documentary, or start a new restaurant. Without your initial experience as a waiter in a restaurant, you would never have found this new calling. In each case, once you open the door to a particular destination, you reveal a set of paths that you probably didn't know existed. In fact, before it's your cause, it's likely something about which you knew nothing.

Love at first sight is rare in most aspects of life. The more experience you have with a person, a profession, or a problem, the more passionate and engaged you become. Let's take this comparison further: If you want to get married, the last thing you should do is sit alone, waiting for the phone to ring, or for Prince or Princess Charming to show up at your door. The best chance to find a compatible match is to meet lots of people. Your attitude (affection) follows your actions (dating), not the other way around. Yes, the dating process can be filled with false starts and disappointments, but you will never be successful unless you embrace the process of discovery.

. . .

Discovery is predicated on curiosity. The more curious you are, the more willing you will be to engage in each new experience. The easiest way to tap into your natural curiosity is by asking questions. Instead of accepting everything you see, or bypassing things that don't make sense to you, question everything. Using the earlier example of being a waiter, each day you might question why that day you receive more (or fewer) tips than the day before; why the restaurant is filled with customers of a particular demographic; or why some items on the menu are never ordered. Answering these questions leads to more questions, opens the door to interesting insights, and exercises your curiosity muscles.

Chip Conley, author of *Emotional Equations,* describes curiosity as fertilizer for the mind. He says, "There's lots of evidence to suggest that it's like blood in our veins, an essential, life-affirming emotion that keeps us forever young." We all know that children are naturally curious, asking endless questions, such as why the sky is blue, why water is wet, and why they have to go to bed so early. Unfortunately, that curiosity is often quashed by responses such as, "Because I said so." Instead of answering flippantly, we would do well to use these questions as a springboard, encouraging children to find out the answers for themselves. (We can do this as adults, too, by looking up answers or performing experiments.) For example, the child who doesn't know why he or she should go to sleep so early could run an experiment to see how the body feels after getting differing amounts of sleep. Learning to answer your own questions—whether you are young or old—fuels curiosity, imagination, and confidence.

Scott Barry Kaufman, the scientific director of the Imagination Institute at the University of Pennsylvania, focuses on the measurement and development of intelligence and creativity. In a recent article, titled "From Evaluation to Inspiration," he discusses the importance of training yourself to be curious and inspired by the world. He writes:

> Inspiration awakens us to new possibilities by allowing us to transcend our ordinary experiences and limitations. Inspiration propels a person from apathy to possibility, and transforms the way we perceive our own capabilities. Inspiration may sometimes be overlooked because of its elusive nature. . . . But as recent research shows, inspiration can be activated, captured, and manipulated, and it has a major effect on important life outcomes.

Scott goes on to outline the things we can do to boost our ability to be inspired, including being open to new experiences, having a positive attitude, surrounding ourselves with inspiring role models, and recognizing the power of inspiration in our lives. Essentially, curiosity and inspiration are mind-sets that we can control. By fueling those mind-sets, we unlock countless opportunities.

My colleagues, Bill Burnett and Dave Evans teach a course at Stanford called "Designing Your Life." In it they help young people unlock their curiosity and imagination, while providing tools for exploring and evaluating the possibilities in front of them. Bill and Dave provide students with a set of tools for reframing and prototyping alternative visions for their career, and bring in a wide range of people to share their professional journeys. This exposes the students to an incredible array of possible paths. Their final project involves crafting three completely different versions of their next five years. The students learn that it is up to them to invent their own future, and that they have the power to choose which vision to make real. They also learn that one's path is rarely straight, and there is a complex dance between vision and revision, based on our unfolding experiences.

## Engage ←→ Envision

There have been many times in my life that I, like Scott Harrison, have looked for a new direction. In each case, I applied to seemingly endless organizations, and with each application I imagined what it would be like to work there, knowing that each opportunity would open up a brand-new world of opportunities. Would I end up in a laboratory, a corporate office, a classroom, or on an expedition boat? Any and all of these were possible.

Sixteen years ago, I stumbled upon the job description for the assistant director role at the Stanford Technology Ventures Program (STVP), the then-new entrepreneurship center at the Stanford School of Engineering. It sounded intriguing, but I crumpled up the job description and threw it in the trash. You see, I had much more experience than was required for the position, and the salary was really low.

The next day, I pulled the piece of paper out of the trash and flattened it. Why not apply? It couldn't hurt, right? As it turns out, the more I learned through the interview process, the more fascinated I became with the opportunity, and I was fortunate enough to be offered the job. Despite the lower level of the role, I would get a chance to work with an amazing group of people on an exciting new initiative.

Once in the door, I soaked up everything I could about entrepreneurship and innovation. I volunteered for more and more projects, building my knowledge and experience. The more I learned, the more opportunities unfolded. Over the years, together with my colleagues, we launched new courses, developed international partnerships, and built an online platform to share our content. Based on the success of these initiatives, we raised funds to grow our team, allowing STVP to continue to grow. I wrote books based on what I'd learned, and was rewarded in many ways, including the chance to travel around the world, sharing what we had done and helping others build their entrepreneurship programs.

None of these roles was in the initial job description; they developed over the years, with more and more engagement.

And nobody gave me that road map—I had to create it my-self. In fact, when you get a job—any job—you aren't given just *that* job, but rather the keys to the building. It's up to you to decide where they will take you.

I've often wondered what would have happened if I had been given the keys to a different building. What I do know is that each one would have held a world of possibilities wait-ing to be discovered. As I walk across the Stanford campus now, I often think of all the other disciplines that would have sparked my imagination, from education reform to climate change. Had I walked through a different door, an entirely different, and equally stimulating, path would have emerged.

Over the years I've learned that everything is interesting once you approach it with an attitude of curiosity. Right after graduate school, I spent two years in a management consult-ing firm. As a junior associate, I was put on any project that needed a warm body, irrespective of my interest or exper-tise. At different times, I was on a team focused on nuclear power plant construction, on telecommunications infra-structure, and on compensation plans for hospital manage-ment. In each case, I walked in cold and learned about the field. Within a few weeks, it was clear that each one of these areas was fascinating, steeped in historical and social con-text, complicated by technical requirements, and full of op-portunities for improvement.

This developing interest is similar to what happens when you watch a movie or read a book. In most cases, you're introduced to characters that are completely different from those you'd ever meet in your everyday life, including an alien from another planet, a person with a unique disability, someone who lives in a different time or place, or even an animal. Within minutes, you enter their world, learn about the challenges they face, gain empathy for them, and care about their fate. The same is true in any discipline: the more immersed you get and the more curious you are, the more interesting it becomes and the more opportunities you see.

Essentially, engagement is the first step to imagining what could be. It requires actively immersing yourself, not just observing from afar. Immersion and curiosity reveal insights and opportunities that are hidden in plain view. If your objective is to identify a goal and to make progress in accomplishing it, the first step is to actively engage. This allows you to mindfully experience each moment, observe useful patterns, and uncover opportunities. No matter where you are in your life, you can always return to this first principle. Engagement is a master key that opens up any door.

## Projects

1. Spend an hour silently observing in one location. It can be anywhere—a café, your office, a city street, a park, or at home. Make as many observations as possible. Consider the implications of these observations, and identify as many opportunities for improvement as you can.

2. Look up job listings in your area, even if you have a job. Select three completely different jobs and write a paragraph that describes the possible paths forward, starting with the advertised role.

# Chapter 2

# Envision

## *All the World's a Stage*

W hat does racecar driving have to do with imagination? Everything. That's certainly the case for Julia Landauer. In preparing for a race, she spends countless hours conjuring up the experience in her mind, including the details of each curve and the optimum path around the track. She visualizes the perfect race, what it will feel like to win, and the roar of the crowd when she stands in the winner's circle.

The act of envisioning every detail is a key to bringing Julia's goals to fruition. She mastered this skill while a student at Stanford. During those years she had much less time to race than her competitors, and was concerned that she would fall behind them in training. Having convinced herself that she wasn't going to let that get in her way, she compensated for her lack of time at the track by spending focused time visualizing the experience she would have had if she'd had the time to race. She created personal mantras that would get her in the correct mind-set, and "trigger words" she could use to relax.

Julia drew upon twelve years of racing experience as she visualized, in exquisite detail, each of the races, so when she did get back into the car, she didn't skip a beat. She won her first race of the season two weeks after she returned. Julia continues to use this technique, even when she has time to train on each racecourse. Days before a race, she starts to visualize the experience so that, at the time of the actual event, she has already won the race countless times in her mind.

Julia's passion for racing began when she was ten years old. As she was growing up in New York City with her sister, her parents looked around for a sport for the entire family. They chose go-kart racing, which could be enjoyed by both boys and girls together. After a couple years of experience, Julia knew that she was happiest when she was on the track. She loved racing, and found that with practice she was able to excel.

When she was twelve, Julia read an article about a boy who was racing cars, not just go-karts. He provided instant motivation, and she decided it was time for her to tackle car racing too. It took another year before she was allowed to drive racecars, since she was still too small to see over the car's dashboard. A year after that, at fourteen, she won her first racecar championship.

This story is meaningful in many ways. It reinforces the message of the previous chapter: that only by engaging do you unlock your passions. Had Julia never set foot in a go-kart, she wouldn't have known that racing was her sport. And then, once she did have that initial experience, it was up to her to envision the next steps, from winning each race to becoming a professional racecar driver.

Athletes of all types use mental imagery as they prepare to tackle physical challenges. Below is a short summary by psychologist Angie LeVan, describing this behavior:

> Noted as one form of mental rehearsal, visualization has been popular since the Soviets started using it back in the 1970s to compete in sports. Now, many athletes employ this technique, including Tiger Woods who has been using it since his pre-teen years. Seasoned athletes use vivid, highly detailed internal images and run-throughs of the entire performance, engaging all their senses in their mental rehearsal, and they combine their knowledge of the sports venue with mental rehearsal.

She quotes golfer Jack Nicklaus as saying, "I never hit a shot, not even in practice, without having a very sharp in-focus picture of it in my head." Heavyweight champion

Muhammad Ali also "used different mental practices to enhance his performance," including the well-known affirmation "I am the greatest."

The ability to visualize is critically important for imagination. Unfortunately, as we get older, most of us aren't encouraged to practice this skill. Beyond childhood, we stop telling imaginative stories ourselves and focus instead on reading other people's fiction; we stop making artwork and begin looking at other people's creations.

Artist Kevin Meier, who runs Flint Books, is doing his best to reverse this trend. He has begun crafting books in which readers make up their own stories. Each book has thirty pages and ten wacky illustrations. It's up to each reader to craft the tale that links the images together. The sample illustration on the next page shows a man surrounded by books and socks. The reader, as writer, gets to determine who the man is and what's going on.

Kevin developed the books to exercise children's imagination. He found that the stories kids craft in response to the images are wonderfully diverse. For example, when shown the image on the page 41, one boy told the tale of a man who desperately wanted to go camping, and another crafted a story about a pirate looking for an island inhabited by wild cheetahs. They each created something fresh and imaginative from the same starting material.

We all have the ability to come up with wildly imaginative ideas when prompted to do so. Unfortunately, we don't get many chances to do this. Instead, we are given problems

with a "right" answer, and are fearful of the consequences if we get the answer "wrong." This tendency toward guarding against consequences is echoed in an experiment conducted by Elad Segev and Odelia Kohn-Oppenheim, gifted-student educators in Israel. They gave third-grade students an extra-credit question at the end of a test. In some cases the question said, "Those who complete the painting the right way will get a point." In other cases, the prompt said only, "Complete the painting." In both cases, the students were presented with a simple triangle.

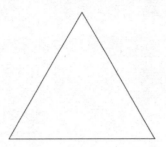

Among students asked to complete the painting the "right" way in return for extra credit, 80 percent drew a simple house, with the triangle as the roof, and on average used only two colors. Those asked just to "complete the painting," on the other hand, came up with a huge array of drawings. None drew a house, and on average those students used five different colors. The examples shown below are taken from a short video about the project.

So many of the "prompts" we get in life unwittingly stifle free expression and imagination. For example, consider the difference between a box of paints and a tablet of blank paper, versus those same paints and a coloring book. Or the difference between a box of Legos without a book of instructions, and one that comes with pages of directions about how to build a predesigned castle or rocket ship.

In the 1970s, the Lego company sold its colorful, interlocking bricks without specific instructions: they were designed for open-ended imagination. Over the years, Lego started selling more kits designed to build specific structures, and the company clearly differentiated those that were geared toward boys versus girls. The following letter to parents came with boxes of Legos back in 1974. This note recently went viral on social media as people remembered the days when this toy wasn't sold with "one right answer":

To Parents:

The urge to create is equally strong in all children. Boys and girls. It's imagination that counts. Not skill. You build whatever comes into your head, the way you want it. A bed or a truck. A dolls house or a spaceship. A lot of boys like dolls houses. They're more human than spaceships. A lot of girls prefer spaceships. They're more exciting than dolls houses. The most important thing is to put the right material in their hands and let them create whatever appeals to them.

Over the years, Lego whittled away at this ode to imagination by offering predesigned kits with the finished product pictured on the box. Once children saw the awesome spaceship or pirate ship designed by Lego engineers, their own imagination was inhibited and they dutifully followed the instructions. This might have been a great business decision by Lego, but it was a huge blow to the millions of children who missed an opportunity for open-ended imagination.

Imagination isn't just child's play. We use our imagination to envision the landscape of our own life. The more imaginative we are, the more vividly we can conjure a landscape of possible paths. With a limited imagination, we're doomed to incremental thinking, doing the same thing as everyone else, with limited variation.

A robust imagination sets the stage for extraordinary accomplishments. Consider Jeff Bezos, founder and CEO of Amazon. He envisioned running an enormous enterprise with global reach when he launched the company in 1995. He named the firm Amazon after the largest river in the world and a legendary nation of female warriors in Greek mythology. The name was deliberately chosen to telegraph that his small startup business was going to be larger than life.

Or consider Martin Luther King's famous "I Have a Dream" speech. That dream of racial equality—his vision for the future—set the stage for an entire social movement. He shared his vision of a time when "my four little children will one day live in a nation where they will not be judged by the color of their skin, but by the content of their character."

It's up to each of us to create our own dream for ourselves. A compelling example comes from a former Stanford student, Kai Kight. He's a classically trained violinist who recently realized that he was playing out someone else's dream for him. After his mother was diagnosed with breast cancer, it became clear that she wouldn't likely be able to fulfill her dream of running a jewelry store. This motivated Kai to take control of his destiny and to craft the future *he* wanted now. Building on his classical music training, he started composing and performing his own unique music. The response to his creations has been wonderful, and he has been given many opportunities to perform. This affirming response has reinforced the message that he is master of his own dreams. These insights are shared in his TEDx talk called "Composing Your World."

Envisioning a bold future is just as important for companies that want to stay relevant in an ever-changing world as it is for individuals. This is why firms such as Google encourage imaginative thinking. Larry Page, Google CEO, is known for his enthusiastic support of "moon shots"—that is, bold projects that have the potential to be legendary. In an interview with *Wired* magazine in 2013, Larry Page described his thinking:

[I]ncremental improvement is guaranteed to be obsolete over time. Especially in technology, where you know there's going to be non-incremental change. . . . So a big part of my job is to get people focused on things that are not just incremental. Take Gmail. When we released that, we were a search company—it was a leap for us to put out an email product, let alone one that gave users 100 times as much storage as they could get anywhere else. That is not something that would have happened naturally if we had been focusing on incremental improvements.

In a more recent interview in *Fortune,* Larry Page described some of the firm's newest moon shots, including robotics, delivery drones, automated homes, glucose-monitoring contact lenses, and drugs to fend off aging. He is looking for "zero-million-dollar research problems"—challenges that no one else in the world is working on. He is an ardent believer in computer scientist Alan Kay's philosophy that "the best way to predict the future is to invent it."

Felipe Santos, a professor at INSEAD, a global graduate business school, earned his PhD at Stanford. His graduate work focused on how firms define the boundaries of their businesses. He described how those boundaries determine the opportunities that each firm identifies. Just like each of us, companies are blind to opportunities that don't fit within the artificial borders they build around their business. For example, had Google defined its business only as an online search firm, it would never have developed self-driving cars;

if Amazon had seen itself only as a bookseller, it would never have set up its web services business; and if Facebook were purely a social network, it would never have entered the virtual reality space.

This is critically important: the boundaries you define are self-imposed, and are limited by what you imagine for yourself. Whether you are running a race, a political campaign, or a company, the vision you have for yourself defines what you can accomplish. This is true whether your vision is modest or monumental. Imagination sets the stage for your journey. By seeing the destination, you reveal the path toward it. Those who run for president of the United States, act on Broadway, or swim across the English Channel all begin with a target—an image of something that has not yet happened—long before it comes to be. As Albert Einstein said, "Imagination is everything. It is the preview of life's coming attractions."

We each make the decision—actively or passively—about the stage on which we will play out our lives. For some, the stage is their family, and for others it is their school or company; for some it is the local community, and for others it is a global stage. Each stage allows us to see the world differently, as well as our place in it. And at any time we can change our vision for the stage on which we are currently playing out our lives.

For example, if you invented a brand-new cookie, you could bake some and enjoy them yourself and share them with your family. You could pack up boxes of cookies and give them to your friends. You could sell them at the local farmers' market, open a cookie store in your neighborhood, or even build a chain of cookie stores around the country or the world. Your stage will grow as you increase the reach and impact you want to have. The vision you have is a prerequisite for what you will achieve. If your goal is to have a successful cookie store in your community, then you will be satisfied with that result. Alternatively, if you have your sights set on running a global cookie business, then you will see and seize the opportunities to make that happen.

This is exactly what happened for Nancy Mueller, who founded Nancy's Specialty Foods in Palo Alto, California, in 1977. She began making large batches of mini-quiches for her own holiday parties. They were so tasty that she was encouraged by friends to sell them. Taking on their challenge, Nancy started selling quiches locally, distributing them in boxes out of a freezer in the back of her car. She could have stopped there, but she didn't. Encouraged by her success, Nancy broadened her vision for the business, which continued to grow, along with her sales. By 1993, Nancy's Special Foods employed 250 people, racked up sales of $30 million a year, and offered products through many national grocery store chains, including Safeway, Giant, and Farm Fresh. Eventually, Nancy sold the business to Heinz Foods, which continues to sell Nancy's Quiches. Essentially, over time Nancy increased her vision of the size of the stage on which she was playing, allowing her to identify new opportunities she would never have seen on a smaller stage.

. . .

I know what it's like to be both driven and limited by my own vision. In 1991, after my first book was released, I saw a need for a better way to help readers find books of interest, including mine. My book, *The Epicurean Laboratory*, was on the chemistry of cooking. Unfortunately, it ended up in the cookbook aisle of the bookstore, as opposed to the science aisle, where most of those who would consider this book interesting would find it.

This problem inspired me to start a multimedia company that helped match books with buyers. I developed an interactive kiosk for use in bookstores that allowed shoppers to look for books by subject, author, or title, and called the product BookBrowser. (Note that this was 1991, several years before web browsers were invented.) Though I had no experience running a technology company, my goal was to develop and deliver the product, and build an organization that was successful enough to be sold in two years.

That's exactly what happened: I built the business and sold it two years later. In retrospect, there was substantially more potential for this business than I had imagined. My limited goal, however, limited the opportunities I saw. If my goal had been to build a large, sustainable business, I would have been much more likely to create new opportunities, hire people who were able to help me scale the venture, and push through the challenges that precipitated the sale of the company. All founders face obstacles. However, only those founders who envision a future where those challenges have been resolved have a high probability of successfully addressing them. As Henry Ford said, "Obstacles are those frightful things you see when you take your eyes off your goal."

Those who can't visualize a path to success are doomed to give up long before those who know that they *will* find a solution. My colleague Steve Blank, who has been on the founding team of eight companies, says that he creates a vision for what he wants to accomplish and then methodically removes all the obstacles in the way. When I look back on BookBrowser, I recognize that there were many ways I could have removed the challenges I faced before I sold my firm. Back then, though, I was limited by my view of what I could accomplish. My vision for the company and for myself framed the scope of the opportunity for me.

The great news is that what we envision for ourselves is completely malleable and can be altered in an instant. That's what happened to Ann Miura-Ko. Ann grew up in Palo Alto, California, the daughter of a scientist, and assumed that she would become a doctor or a research scientist. She studied electrical engineering at Yale, and while there, she took a position in the dean's office, doing administrative work to help pay for college.

On a winter day in 1992, the dean asked Ann if she would give a tour of the engineering school to a visitor. During the tour, her guest learned that Ann was from Palo Alto and offered her a chance to shadow him at work when she returned home over spring break. Ann asked him what he did, and he said that he was the president of Hewlett-Packard. Intrigued, she accepted Lew Platt's invitation.

While shadowing Platt at Hewlett Packard, Ann got to see him in action, running meetings, and making decisions. At one point, Lew suggested that they get a picture together in his office, with Ann sitting across from him on a white couch. A few weeks later, a letter arrived in the mail with the photo of Ann and Lew, plus another photo taken the same week in the same room. This time, instead of Ann, Lew Platt was sitting across from Bill Gates, president of Microsoft as they signed a joint agreement.

Ann looked at the two photographs taken from the same angle in the same room, with both guests sitting on the same couch. At that moment she saw her life differently. The walls of her future opened up, and she visualized herself as the leader of a global company. She was bright and driven, but had never considered that she could play out her life on a global stage. Everything changed in that instant.

Flash forward to 2015. Ann is now a partner at Floodgate Fund in Palo Alto, which she cofounded with Mike Maples in 2010 after earning a Ph.D. in engineering at Stanford. She spends her days guiding early-stage startups that are having a global impact, and has been recognized as one of the most influential leaders in Silicon Valley.

As Ann's story illustrates, most people don't question the stage on which they live, or don't feel comfortable expanding the scope of their impact. Yet a single instant can change their view. A conversation, a book, a movie, or even a photograph can shift your perspective on how you envision your life unfolding.

Michael Tubbs is another terrific example of that. Growing up in the 1990s in Stockton, California, he was the son of a teenage mother and a father who was incarcerated. The city, riddled with crime and unemployment, was very poor. Despite this challenging start, Michael set his sights high and excelled in school, earning admission to Stanford. While doing an internship in Washington, DC, Michael received a call from his mother telling him that his cousin had been murdered back home. In that instant, Michael felt compelled to drive changes in his own local community, and he decided to run for local office.

Michael initially thought that he'd need years of work experience and more education before running for political office. He learned, however, that all he needed was to be over eighteen years old and to receive over 50 percent of the vote. So, while still a student at Stanford, Michael ran for city council in Stockton and won, becoming the youngest elected official in the city's history. He has been in office for two years and has already installed several new programs to fight crime and encourage young people to complete school.

Congresswoman Anna Eshoo is a gripping example of someone who expanded the scope of her vision for herself much later in life. Raised in Connecticut, her immigrant parents instilled in their children the responsibilities of citizenship and love of country at an early age. Little did she realize that one day she would run for and win one of the highest offices in the country.

In 1979, Eshoo applied for a fellowship with the prestigious CORO Foundation in San Francisco, which educates individuals on how communities are structured. Her public sector internship was in the office of Leo T. McCarthy, the then-Speaker of the California Assembly and a future mentor, who encouraged Eshoo to run for elective office—an idea she had never entertained.

In 1982, Eshoo took the leap, and ran for an open seat on the San Mateo County Board of Supervisors. She won and served on the Board for ten years. With a successful legislative record, in 1988, Eshoo was again encouraged to run, this time for Congress, a suggestion she thought was comparable to running for president! The idea stretched her thinking and she finally decided to take the leap onto this larger stage. She ran for Congress and lost to Tom Campbell by just 2 percentage points. In 1992, Tom Campbell vacated the seat to run for the U.S. Senate. Eshoo ran again, won that election, and was first sworn into the U.S. House of Representatives in January 1993.

Congresswoman Eshoo told me that at each stage she had to "dig deep" to reach a decision, slay a lot of personal demons, and work on her confidence before moving to a larger stage. Every day in Congress is filled with pressing domestic and foreign issues, from energy to human rights, health care, biomedical research, technology, and our national economy.

Eshoo translates her legislative work to her constituents and reads everything they send to her. Every long-fought legislative win propels her to the next set of challenges.

Congresswoman Eshoo's success echoes research showing that visualization of what you hope to accomplish is not enough. In fact, it can even backfire! You need not only to imagine the future you hope to reach, but also to envision the obstacles you need to overcome along the way.

Scientists Heather Barry Kappes at New York University and Gabriele Oettingen at the University of Hamburg found that indulging in positive fantasies about a desired future actually predicts poor performance. The two researchers' experiments demonstrated that visualizing an attractive outcome led to lower energy in the subjects. Kappes and Oettingen hypothesize that the lower energy, as measured both physiologically and psychologically, reduces the drive needed to achieve one's goals. Thus they suggest that visualizing *both* the outcome *and* what needs to be done to reach that goal is critical to mustering the energy needed to succeed. Put bluntly, you can't just be a dreamer; your big dreams must include a realistic understanding of what you need to do to reach them. The Invention Cycle provides a framework for just that by elucidating the attitudes and actions needed to bring your dreams to life.

For many, reaching for a large goal is scary. Sometimes, we don't believe that we belong on that larger stage and fear that we will be found to be unworthy of the role. Known as the impostor syndrome, this feeling of being a fraud and not deserving the success we have achieved is surprisingly common. Up to 70 percent of people experience impostor syndrome at some time in their lives. It is remarkable that so many people feel that they are on stages that are too big, and that they don't belong.

As Olivia Fox Cabane told students at Stanford in our Entrepreneurial Thought Leaders lecture series:

> In the impostor syndrome, people feel that they don't really know what they're doing, and it's just a matter of time before they're found out and exposed as a fraud. This syndrome is estimated to hit 70 percent to 80 percent of the population. And it hits the highest levels of business and education. Every time I speak about this at Harvard, at Yale, at Stanford, and at MIT, the room goes so silent you could hear a pin drop. And then the students breathe a sigh of relief at hearing that this has a name and they're not the only ones to have felt it. I've heard that every time the incoming class of Stanford Business School is asked, "How many of you feel you are the one mistake the admissions committee made?" two-thirds of the students immediately raise their hands.

You can look at these feelings as growing pains. Whenever we move to a larger stage, it feels somewhat uncomfortable. There are those who have been there much longer and look pretty comfortable in that position. They too were new once, however, and felt just as awkward. When you're stretching to a larger role, or bigger stage, it's helpful to acknowledge the things you don't know, to ask for help, and to realize that everyone feels (or has felt) the same way. Confidence comes from experience, not the other way around. The world is filled with people who serve as examples of what can be accomplished. You'll find that each of them has scaled hurdles to reach their objectives—in fact, the larger the goal, the higher the hurdles they have overcome.

If your objective is to achieve something of merit, you need to begin with a clear vision of your goal. That vision, as described in the previous chapter, is inextricably tied to your experiences. This is the essence of imagination: by actively engaging in the world, you identify problems and opportunities and then envision how you might address them. All great ventures and adventures begin with imagination. This, in turn, leads to the next stage in the Invention Cycle—creativity. It is here that you apply your imagination to address your chosen challenge. The following two chapters delve into the importance of motivation and experimentation in unlocking the pathway toward those goals.

## Projects

1. Make up your own story, using the illustration by Kevin Meier on page 41.

2. Think of the world as a collection of stages, from your hometown to the entire world. Which stage are you on right now, and which one do you want to play out your life on in the future? Return to the letter that you wrote earlier and edit it if needed to reflect any new goals.

3. Pick a role that you currently have and imagine the stage expanding. What would the role look like on a grander stage? What would you need to do to stretch to a larger platform?

4. What are the hurdles on the road to your objective? Which ones are external and which are internal?

# Part Two

# Creativity

## *Motivate and Experiment*

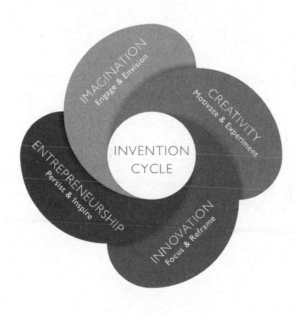

My parents are fans of the opera, and they count my lack of enthusiasm for this art form as a big disappointment. More broadly, they look around the audience at the performances they attend and see row upon row of listeners with gray hair; and were saddened when the New York City Opera, which opened in 1943, closed its doors due to bankruptcy in 2013. Aging patrons is a daunting problem for all the traditional arts, including theater, ballet, and classical music. Performers and patrons alike wonder where the future audiences for these long-lived forms of entertainment will come from. Like any problem, this is an opportunity for creative thinking.

The world of entertainment has changed dramatically over the years, and creative companies are looking at this as a chance to shake things up, knowing that if they don't, they face certain demise. A deep motivation and commitment to solving this problem has led to a lot of exciting experimentation. This is the crux of creativity—*tapping into your motivation to address an opportunity, and then experimenting until you find a solution.* Creativity builds upon imagination.

Nothing will happen with your imagined goals unless you are motivated to experiment to come up with creative ways to reach them.

The Cleveland Orchestra is a case in point. This organization set the goal to attract the youngest audience in its history by its one hundredth birthday in 2018. This world-class orchestra needed creative ways to bring new fans to the concert hall. To get this effort started, supporters launched a Center for Future Audiences, with the mission of reaching listeners from preschool to college. As of 2014, their efforts have increased the number of young people in the hall from 8 percent to 20 percent. They've done this by enlisting the help of young "ambassadors" who promote events, by offering student passes, and by putting on short concerts on Friday evenings, followed by a party.

Creative experimentation to bring more people to the arts doesn't stop there. A theater company in New York acknowledged that many theatergoers are in need of entertainment and a nap! So they decided to invite people to do both. Their show, *Dream of a Red Chamber,* was designed to put people to sleep—the audience members remove their shoes and lounge in beds, surrounded by a cast of actors in elaborate costumes and are lulled by relaxing music. This idea explored what it's like to create music for the third of our lives when we're asleep.

Another experiment turns Shakespeare's *Macbeth* into a multistage event. *Sleep No More,* in New York City, provides an immersive theater experience. This award-winning production invites audience members to move freely through the story, visiting different rooms, each presenting a different scene from the play. Performed in a five-floor building, the show uses dozens of sets, including a lunatic asylum, a doctor's office, bedrooms, a cemetery, and a ballroom. There is no speaking from either the actors or the audience, the audience members all wear masks, and each person's experience of the play is unique.

These are all examples of creativity at work, driven by the *motivation* to make traditional music and theater relevant to younger audiences and the willingness *to experiment* to identify solutions. Some of these experiments take off and are implemented on a larger scale, while others provide valuable data on what works and what doesn't. The next two chapters explore how motivation fuels creative experimentation.

Chapter 3

# Motivate

## *You're the Customer*

D on Wettrick teaches high school in Indiana, and a few years ago he turned his classroom upside down. Having watched a TED talk by author Daniel Pink about motivation, he realized that he was missing an opportunity to tap into his students' passions to drive their own education. Don decided to experiment with Pink's ideas to see what would happen.

Daniel Pink's framework, described in his book *Drive: The Surprising Truth About What Motivates Us,* outlines three keys to motivation: autonomy, mastery, and purpose. *Autonomy* means selecting what you do, how you do it, and with whom you work. *Mastery* involves the opportunity to succeed at tasks that are hard enough to be challenging, but not so hard as to be frustrating. *Purpose* provides individuals a chance to work on something that they feel is important.

Using Pink's model, and inspiration from Google's and 3M's approach of encouraging their employees to spend a percentage of their time on their own projects, Don gives his students a full class period each day to work on a project of their choice. The ultimate goal is to give the students a chance to learn how to tap into their own motivation to chart their learning. The results are impressive.

At the beginning of the course, Don invites the students to select their own project. After years of reacting to other people's assignments for them, many find it a struggle to pick a topic. To help them all get going, Don turns the first two weeks of the course over to brainstorming about opportunities in their midst, allowing even the most anxious students to find something that sparks their interest. Students realize that by paying attention—as discussed in the chapter on engagement—there are opportunities to make a difference everywhere. The students soon identify long lists of challenges to be addressed in their classroom, school, and the broader community.

There are a few rules in Don's course. 1) The students need to submit a formal proposal for their project. 2) They have to collaborate with outside experts in the field. 3) They need to create blog posts using text and video to share their accomplishments and the surprises along the way. 4) At the end of the project, each student or team is required to present what they did to a group of stakeholders and then negotiate with Don for a grade for the project. (Some students choose to work on their projects independently, and others work in teams of two or three.)

Many of the teams decide to tackle local issues within their school. Projects have included helping special needs students launch a coffee shop to get them more involved with the community; developing an environmentally friendly plan for maintaining the school grounds; and helping a fellow classmate who was depressed and overweight gain control of his life. Other projects have more far reaching goals. For example, Jared is currently working on a transparent solar cell and has several different versions of a product that he plans to produce and sell. Mikaela has designed an educational toy that she has prototyped and tested. And Jessica is currently focusing on cutting down on light pollution in her town.

For each of the projects, the students make a plan, reach out to those whose buy-in they need, seek input and guidance from experts, figure out how to work around obstacles in their way, and share their experience with the world. In the course of the project, the students realize that their personal motivation is an important ingredient, driving their project forward. The more motivated they are to address the problem, the more effort they put into finding solutions.

This type of experience isn't available to most students. In fact, as discussed in the chapter on imagination, most of us are instructed to blindly follow the path someone else has set, given predetermined assignments with one right answer. Even outside the classroom, most people get both direct and subtle messaging about what is expected of them. Many wake up one day, deep into their career, and realize that they've been following someone else's dream, not their own. The problem with following someone else's plan is that it doesn't tap into your own internal motivation. Your motivation is the fuel that refills your tank, propelling you forward and providing resilience when the going gets rough.

For years I've been reminding students in my classes that *they* are the "customer"—not I. I point out that after years of pleasing their teachers, their parents, and those who craft standardized exams, it is time for each of them to make their own choices about what they want to get out of their experience at school and beyond, driven by their own interests. Clearly, there are consequences for their choices, but it is up to each of them to make those choices. For example, if they want to spend all their time on an extracurricular project that's really meaningful to them, go for it! If they want to stay in their dorm room writing computer code for their startup, why not? Yes, their grades might suffer, but that is *their* choice to make, not mine. We each need to learn how to tap into our internal motivations and not be led exclusively by external drivers, such as what other people want us to do.

This resonates with recent research by Amy Wrzesniewski of Yale and Barry Schwartz of Swarthmore. They studied the interplay of internal and external (also known as instrumental) motivation. Internal motivation comes from your personal drive to accomplish a goal, independent of what others think, while external motivation comes from outside validation, such as rewards and recognition. For most people, and most activities, there is a balance between internal and external motivation.

The objective of Wrzesniewski and Schwartz's research was to determine if there is an optimum balance between the two types of motivation for optimal success. These scientists surveyed over eleven thousand cadets in the entering class of the U.S. Military Academy at West Point to determine what motivated them to enter the academy. They looked at factors such as the desire to be a leader, which is an internal motivation, and the hope of getting a good job, which is an external motivation.

After several years, the researchers tracked down the graduates to see what they were doing. They found a fascinating interplay between internal and external motivation, as described below:

> We found, unsurprisingly, that the stronger their internal reasons were to attend West Point, the more likely cadets were to graduate and become commissioned officers. Also unsurprisingly, cadets with internal motives did better in the military (as evidenced by early promotion recommendations) than did those without internal motives and were also more likely to stay in the military after their five years of mandatory service—unless (and

this is the surprising part) they also had strong instrumental motives.

Remarkably, cadets with strong internal and strong instrumental motives for attending West Point performed worse on every measure than did those with strong internal motives but weak instrumental ones. They were less likely to graduate, less outstanding as military officers and less committed to staying in the military.

The implications of this finding are significant. Whenever a person performs a task well, there are typically both internal and instrumental consequences. . . . Helping people focus on the meaning and impact of their work, rather than on, say, the financial returns it will bring, may be the best way to improve not only the quality of their work but also—counterintuitive though it may seem—their financial success.

I've seen this play out closer to home. Each year our twelve STVP Mayfield Fellows work in a startup company over the summer. This is part of a nine-month work-study program that focuses on entrepreneurial leadership. The students spend the spring quarter learning about startup strategies and organizational behavior. Then during that summer each works at a startup firm where he or she hosts an open house for his or her classmates. During the fall quarter they each present a case study on one key aspect of their summer employment experience.

A few years ago, as I sat through the company presentation for a firm that made a mobile advertising application, I realized that it wasn't clear what was driving the business. There didn't appear to me to be an overarching mission for the company; they didn't seem to be addressing a specific problem. In fact, the founder spent most of his time talking about money. Genuinely curious, I politely asked the founder what motivated him. This question clearly flustered him, and his answer left me in the dark. It wasn't surprising to any of us when the company folded only a few months later. It was clear that the founder didn't have the meaningful motivation needed to sustain his business through the inevitable challenges.

As a result of this interaction, at each subsequent company open house one of the Mayfield Fellows could be counted on to ask the company founder about his or her motivation. The range and depth of the responses were spectacular. It was abundantly clear to all of us which company leaders had thought about this question before and which had not. As one student wrote in her reflections on this experience, "After meeting a dozen different CEOs throughout the summer, it is clear that there is no recipe for becoming a perfect leader. The common denominator was those who are successful all had a clear vision for the future of the venture and were able to motivate others to work tirelessly towards these goals."

The linkage between motivation and success resonates with a lesson from Guy Kawasaki, former Apple "evangelist," technology investor, and prolific author on entrepreneurship.

He has observed that companies with a strong mission are much more likely to succeed than those that are focused only on money. The quote below is from a talk Guy gave at Stanford as part of the Entrepreneurial Thought Leader lecture series:

> The first thing I figured out and learned, sometimes the hard way, about entrepreneurship is that the core, the essence of entrepreneurship is about making meaning. Many, many people start companies to make money, the quick flip, the dot-com phenomenon. And I have noticed in both the companies that I've started and funded and been associated with, that those companies that are fundamentally founded to change the world, to make the world a better place, to make meaning, are the companies that make a difference. They are the companies to succeed.

Back in the classroom in the Fall, after their internships, the Mayfield Fellows get a chance to explore what motivates each of them. Going around the room, my colleague Tom Byers and I ask each student to share what drives them. They realize pretty quickly that this is a really hard question to answer. Our motivations are complex and multifaceted. There are obvious motivations, such as safety, health, friendship, and financial security, as well as less conspicuous drivers based on our individual background, hardships, and inspirations.

One of our frequent class guests is Scott Kriens, the former CEO of Juniper Networks. In this role he had a chance to interview hundreds of people as potential hires for the company. Instead of asking the candidates about their experience, he tells our students, he always starts with a simple question: "Who are you?" The question is designed to uncover what drives the interviewee. Going around the room, each of the Mayfield Fellows answers this same question, again realizing just how challenging it is. There are myriad answers, each revealing another layer of what motivates each of us.

Most of the time our motivation evolves over time, but sometimes it is jump-started by a singular event. That's what happened for Marie Johnson. She was a Ph.D. student studying biomedical engineering at the University of Minnesota. She had a four-year-old daughter and was pregnant with her second child.

Marie was working on a research project with scientists at 3M to design a computerized stethoscope that would give a much more detailed analysis of heart valve function. While learning how to operate the stethoscope, she used her husband as a test subject, collecting data on him over the course of several months.

Horribly, a year into the project, Marie's husband died suddenly of a heart attack right after leaving the gym. Nobody would have suspected that he had a heart problem. On the outside he looked perfectly healthy—at forty-one he was six foot two and weighed 180 pounds. It took an autopsy to reveal that three of the arteries in his heart were blocked.

This cataclysmic event mobilized Marie to understand what had happened and to develop a way to identify these types of blockages long before someone suffers a heart attack. Within one week of her husband's death, she started tackling this problem by studying statistics and mathematical modeling so that she could analyze telltale frequency patterns correlated with coronary disease. The data that Marie collected from her late husband served to jump-start her analysis. It shed light on what to look for in someone with coronary heart disease, providing insights into how to detect this life-threatening condition before it's too late.

Marie's company, AUM Cardiovascular, is dedicated to eliminating deaths due to coronary heart disease. Picking up turbulent sounds from the heart using a handheld device that looks like an air hockey paddle, the noninvasive tool is designed to replace a test that costs $1,000 with one that costs only $100, so that many more people can get access to this type of diagnostic testing. Marie has eleven people on her team, including designers and engineers, who are all now equally motivated to address this problem.

Our motivations influence everything we do, but because they are not always obvious, our behavior is sometimes confusing, even to ourselves. In my creativity course I run an exercise designed to reveal insights about each person's motivation. I start by drawing a large two-by-two matrix on the board—Passion on the X axis and Confidence on the Y axis.

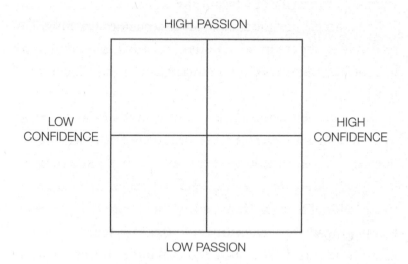

HIGH PASSION

LOW CONFIDENCE

HIGH CONFIDENCE

LOW PASSION

Each student fills out four sticky notes, one for each quadrant, and places them in the relevant square. In the upper-right quadrant they put a pursuit for which they have high passion and high confidence; in the upper-left quadrant they affix one for which they have high passion and low confidence. In the lower quadrants they place an activity for which they have low passion and high confidence and one for which they have low passion and low confidence. For some people this is a really challenging task, since they don't routinely use these terms to consider the tasks in their life.

Once this is done, we discuss the results. It becomes clear that those things in the upper-right quadrant are things we spend considerable time doing. Our active engagement leads to confidence, and confidence reinforces our passion. We are motivated to pursue these activities because it feels great to express our mastery of relevant skills.

For example, for me this quadrant includes teaching. I'm relatively confident in my abilities and am highly motivated to continue improving my knowledge and techniques with practice.

The upper-left quadrant includes things we say we *want* to do, but usually *don't* do. We lack confidence because we don't spend time practicing these skills. Whether the activity is singing, skiing, or learning a new language, there is something holding us back from getting fully engaged. It is only by ramping up our commitment to this task that we will put in the time and effort required to pull it into the upper-right quadrant. For me, this quadrant would include exercise. I'm motivated to stay fit but don't put in nearly enough time to fully reach my objectives.

Those items in the lower-left quadrant represent activities we don't have any interest in pursuing. We are neither passionate nor confident about them. These are great things to outsource to others who enjoy these tasks. For me, this includes paying bills, which I happily outsource to my husband. Alternatively, we can find ways to artificially motivate ourselves. If these are tasks that we *need* to accomplish, there are ways to reframe how we think about them. We can focus on the outcome as opposed to the process, find ways to make the task more pleasurable, or plant rewards along the way.

If I needed to pay the bills, for example, I could put on my favorite music and plan something rewarding for after the task is completed.

The final quadrant includes items for which we have high confidence but low passion. This is the most interesting square since it includes items that we have already mastered but don't enjoy doing. One option is to probe *why* we aren't motivated. For some things, we give up on pushing ourselves once we reach a minimum level of skill or get bored with the repetition. Increasing our motivation allows us to reach the next level of mastery.

An example for me would be cooking, which is a task I used to enjoy quite a bit. After reaching a basic level of skill, however, I stopped learning new recipes and often repeat the same menus. If I were more motivated, I would learn new recipes and techniques. By understanding that the lack of drive is our own choosing, we gain control over how we focus our energy. It is up to each of us to decide if we want to ramp up our commitment for things in the lower-right quadrant.

I've seen people quickly shift from one quadrant to another. For example, several years ago, there was someone on our team at STVP who was doing a truly marginal job. Though clearly very bright and creative, she wasn't putting in the effort to do quality work. Everything she delivered was late and filled with errors. I sat down with her to discuss her performance. The following week, she started doing a terrific job. I was shocked. I asked her what had happened. Her answer was, "I decided to do a good job." The real message was that before that discussion she had decided *not* to do quality work. She was completely capable, but she had chosen to do a sloppy job until she was urged to step up. With the flip of a switch, she changed her attitude and her performance improved.

This can be generalized to all aspects of life. We each choose how we approach every single thing in our life. Consider white light, which is composed of all the other colors in the spectrum. When you use different lenses, you see different colors. It is up to you to choose which lens you use. When we experience anything, from a romantic scene to a barroom brawl, there are elements of every human emotion. It is up to each of us to determine which details we will notice and which emotions we will feel. Just ask a diverse group of people who have experienced the same event to reflect upon it, and you will get a plethora of responses depending on the way each individual chooses to see the world.

I use the word *choose* deliberately, because we are each responsible for choosing the lenses we use. With different lenses on, we see different challenges and opportunities. If you look at the world with an eye toward ways you can address the challenges you face, then that's what you see. If instead your lens casts you as a victim, then that is the part you play. Remember, every problem really is an opportunity; and the bigger the problem, the bigger the opportunity. It's up to each of us to make something out of what we are given. Consider the drawing of the triangle in chapter 2. There are endless ways a person might complete that picture. To quote

John Gardner in a speech he delivered at McKinsey & Company in 1990, "Life is the art of drawing without an eraser." That is, accepting what life gives you and then responding. Gardner went on to say:

> Meaning is not something you stumble across, like the answer to a riddle or the prize in a treasure hunt. Meaning is something you build into your life. You build it out of your own past, out of your affections and loyalties, out of the experience of humankind as it is passed on to you, out of your own talent and understanding, out of the things you believe in, out of the things and people you love, out of the values for which you are willing to sacrifice something. The ingredients are there. You are the only one who can put them together into that unique pattern that will be your life.

It is up to each of us to mine our lives for meaning. A compelling example comes from Khalida Brohi, the founder of the Sughar Empowerment Society in Pakistan. She grew up in a rural village with long-held traditions, including "honor killings" of young women who didn't follow their parents' wishes. If a girl said that she didn't want to marry the man her family had chosen for her, for instance, the community believed that it was acceptable to murder her.

At sixteen, Khalida went back to her village after studying in the capital city of Karachi, and found that one of her closest friends had been killed for her decision to marry the man she loved, not the one her parents had chosen for her. This incident struck Khalida to the core. After experiencing life in the city, where she realized that honor killings are unnecessary and barbaric, she vowed to stand up for women's rights in the region. When interviewed at the Clinton Global Initiative, she said:

> When I was sixteen years old I lost my friend to honor killings. . . . This is it. This means that I am supposed to be doing something for all those women. I was a teenager burning with fire. I knew I was going to save all the women around the world from honor killings.

Khalida founded the Sughar program to empower women by helping them learn a trade that provided some financial independence. (Sughar means "skilled and confident women.") Her aim is to help over one million women over the next ten years. This goal has motivated her to experiment in an effort to come up with the best ways to address the problem of honor killings. She has taken what she was given, no matter how horrible, and created something meaningful.

This last example focuses on an enormous problem, but most issues in our lives are far more mundane. We stumble over metaphorical cracks in the sidewalk all day long. It is our choice to see them as opportunities, as opposed to problems, and commit to addressing them. Just like the children in

Don Wettrick's classroom, we can train ourselves to see and tackle the challenges in our lives as opposed to blindly walking by.

Starting at the beginning of the Invention Cycle, with active engagement and envisioning what might be (imagination), you decide what motivates you and then experiment to come up with solutions (creativity). In the next chapter I discuss how even a small dose of motivation can lead to tiny experiments to address the challenge. The results of those experiments can, in turn, ramp up your motivation, building both your confidence and your passion to further address the challenge. Remember, you choose what motivates you, and even a tiny dose of motivation suffices to get you started!

## Projects

1. What really motivates you? Consider the short term, the intermediate term, and the long term. Think about that question as it relates to different aspects of your life, including family, education, work, and community.

2. Fill out the Passion–Confidence matrix with activities in your life that fit into the four quadrants. Ask friends, family, or colleagues to do the same, and share your results. Discuss why you placed specific items in each quadrant and whether there are ways to move some of the items into the upper-right quadrant.

Chapter 4

# Experiment

## *Break Some Eggs*

Justin Rosenstein was working at Facebook as an engineer and found the experience of collaborating with a large, diverse team very frustrating. Too much time was wasted on "work about work," as Justin describes it, as opposed to getting the intended work done. It took an inordinate amount of time to synchronize the team, making sure that everyone was up to speed and knew how his or her contributions fit into a larger plan. Justin could have spent time complaining. Instead, he addressed the problem head-on by doing some experiments with his team at Facebook.

Justin spent a year inside Facebook building and testing a new teamwork software platform. The tool he developed provided ways for everyone on the team to communicate and collaborate, without wasteful redundancy. It proved so useful that the platform was rolled out across the entire company. Increasingly passionate about this project, Justin—along with Facebook cofounder Dustin Moskovitz—left Facebook to launch Asana, devoting all their efforts to building this tool for other companies. Justin was motivated to increase productivity in organizations of all types.

Initially, Justin had no intention of turning his solution into a new company. But the opportunity evolved as his passion for this problem grew, as did his confidence that he could address it. This is the core of creativity: applying your imagination to address a challenge, and leveraging your motivation to begin experimentation.

In fact, we are *all* experimentation machines. Each time we speak, we're listening for the response and adjusting the conversation accordingly. Each time we try a new product, we're evaluating whether it meets our needs. And each time we taste a new food, we're doing an experiment, determining whether we like it. Instead of relying solely on our instincts to experiment, we can be mindful of this process and experiment with our experimenting. The more thoughtful we are about the tests we do, the more data we collect, and the better we are at adjusting to the results we gather.

This is exactly what Justin and his team at Asana do. Every four months everyone in the company gets together to plan for the coming months. Together they generate a set of high-priority experiments and explicitly evaluate the risks and rewards for each one. Some are big bets with a high potential return, as well as a high risk of failure. Some are incremental improvements to the product that have a high chance of success.

Going even further, for each new project they do a visioning exercise in which they write up fictional summaries of what will happen four months in the future. Also known as "premortems," these take place before the group starts a project (as opposed to postmortem reports, which happen afterward). Premortems help anticipate what might happen before they start work so that they can avoid foreseeable issues and lay a solid foundation for success.

One visioning report describes the wild success they will be celebrating if all goes well, and another outlines all that might go wrong and why a proposed project could fail. This approach allows all involved to fully understand the potential of each experiment they are doing, and uncovers some of the things that might go wrong. The visioning process provides an opportunity to anticipate success and failure, and to address potential potholes before anyone falls into them. At upcoming meetings they review not just the outcomes, but also the processes they used, continually experimenting to get better results.

Thoughtful experimentation, like that described above, is a key part of the creative process, allowing you to move beyond imagination, where you envision possibilities, to creativity, where you begin finding solutions. Experimentation uncovers a wealth of alternatives so that you can evaluate those options.

Children do this naturally as they discover how the world works. Scientists at the University of California at Berkeley and the University of Edinburgh did a study to determine whether preschoolers are more willing than college students to experiment to find solutions. They selected 100 four- and five-year-old children and asked them to turn on a music box that was activated by putting different-shaped pieces of clay on top of the toy. They also tested 170 college students with the same task, and found that the children were much better at this than the adults.

One of the researchers, Alison Gopnik, observed that the children were more likely to try unusual approaches. While being interviewed by Michelle Trudeau on National Public Radio, Gopnik explained:

> This is flexible, fluid thinking—children exploring an unlikely hypothesis. Exploratory learning comes naturally to young children, says Gopnik. Adults, on the other hand, jump on the first, most obvious solution and doggedly stick to it, even if it's not working. That's inflexible, narrow thinking. "We think the moral of the study is that maybe children are better at solving problems when the solution is an unexpected one," says Gopnik.

We can preserve this ability into adulthood by polishing our "pretotyping" skills. This term was coined by Alberto

Savoia, who spent years leading product development teams at high-tech companies and was most recently the "innovation agitator" at Google. This latter role is where he developed his ideas about pretotyping. Alberto observed that most people fall in love with their ideas, dive in, and commit way too much time and money before figuring out whether people actually want what's been proposed. He refers to the pretotyping process as "testing before investing," to figure out if you should make the product in the first place. As Alberto says, "In pretotyping, our assumption is that we are wrong, so we don't really want to act confidently, but cautiously, testing our hypotheses before jumping in."

Most people know the value of prototyping to create samples of what they intend to build. Prototypes allow you to test parameters, such as size, weight, and the overall user experience of products, websites, and services. They are designed to answer questions such as, "Can we build it?"

But what if you're doing the wrong thing in the first place? Pretotypes are made *before* you dive into building prototypes, and are designed to be experiments to determine whether you're even going in the right direction. As Alberto says in his book on pretotyping (which is itself a pretotype!):

Pretotypes make it possible to collect valuable usage and market data to make a go/no-go decision on a new idea at a fraction of the cost of prototypes: hours or days instead of weeks or months, and pennies instead of dollars. Pretotyping helps you fail fast, recover fast and leaves you plenty of time, money, energy and enthusiasm to explore new tweaks or ideas until you hit on something that people seem to want.

There is another important value of pretypes: you don't need much motivation to do a quick experiment. With only a small seed of commitment to an idea, you can do a prototype to see if the idea has wings. Furthermore, since most new ideas fail, it behooves us all to do tests as early as possible to see if we're going in the right direction.

Alberto outlines a set of informative experiments that can be used to give ideas a test drive. Below are a few examples:

*The Mechanical Turk.* With this method, you replace a complicated computation task with a human being. The term originated in Europe in the late eighteenth century. An inventor crafted a mechanical man, dressed in Turkish robes and a turban, that he claimed could play chess. Actually, though, there was a live person under the table who remotely moved the mannequin. This concept is still used today. You can use services, such as Amazon Mechanical Turk, to outsource repetitive tasks that can be done only by humans, such as sorting photos or reviewing transcripts. The Mechanical Turk approach to prototyping is exactly the same—instead of building a complex and expensive tool, you first try it out with a *person* doing the task. For example, instead of designing sophisticated photo recognition software, see whether people want this service by employing a group of kids to do the task for a few bucks.

*The Pinocchio Technique.* This technique involves creating a "wooden" mockup of your idea—that is, you use an inexpensive stand-in. It's great for determining how a product or service might fit into someone's life. A great example comes from an often-used project assigned to middle school students. They are asked to carry around a raw egg in a basket for a week, making sure it doesn't crack. The objective is to give these youngsters a small taste of the experience of being a parent, so that they understand how much work it is to be responsible for a delicate baby twenty-four hours a day. This simple pretotype is incredibly effective in demonstrating how much work it is to care for a baby, without having to enlist and endanger several dozen real infants.

*The Facade.* In this case you advertise a product or service that doesn't yet exist to gauge the level of interest. You can do this by putting test ads online, on the radio, or in a newspaper or a flier and see whether people respond. The response rate is a great indicator of actual interest. A super example comes from Bill Gross, who runs Idealab. Years ago, before e-commerce was well accepted, he wanted to know whether people would buy a car online. He set up a website to sell cars—with nothing but a page that offered cars for sale! Here is the story in Bill Gross's words:

> In 1999, we started CarsDirect. Back then people worried about putting credit cards online; here I wanted to sell a car online! We put a site up on a Wednesday night; by Thursday morning, we had four orders. We quickly

shut the site down (we'd have to buy four cars at retail and deliver them to these four customers at a loss) but proved the thesis. Only then did we start building the real site and company.

The most important goal of all these pretotyping techniques is to gather data. Even when pretotypes don't work out as hoped, they provide valuable lessons that can be applied to the next round of experiments. Because they are done quickly, there is minimal harm done. Since pretotypes don't require much effort, they also don't require a huge commitment. If you approach your life, your education, and your business as a series of experiments, then all results serve as data to inform the *next* round of experiments.

Peter Sims writes about this concept in his book *Little Bets,* in which he shares insights about the experimental processes behind the development of successful products, processes, and organizations. We so often look at finished products and believe that they were born fully formed. This just isn't the case. Whether it's a hilarious comedy routine, a business strategy, or an elegant product, these successes grow out of hard work backed by thoughtful experimentation, making small steps, one at a time. Peter describes the process as follows:

At the core of this experimental approach, little bets are concrete actions taken to discover, test, and develop ideas that are achievable and affordable. They begin as creative possibilities that get iterated and refined over time, and they are particularly valuable when trying to navigate amid uncertainty, create something new, or attend to open-ended problems. When we can't know what's going to happen, little bets help us learn about the factors that can't be understood beforehand. The important thing to remember is that while prodigies are exceptionally rare, anyone can use little bets to unlock creative ideas.

People working with or for others tend to ask for permission before doing an experiment to see whether an idea might work. This sounds like a good plan, but it can backfire. As Rich Cox, my colleague at Stanford's Hasso Plattner Institute of Design (d.school), who runs a consulting firm called People Rocket, so astutely stated, "Asking for permission just transfers the risk to someone else." This is important. If you ask someone to endorse your experiment, you are transferring the risk to them—and that has consequences. Since they aren't directly involved in the experiment's success, they are more likely to pass on taking this risk and tell you not to pursue it. If it's a small bet and you feel comfortable that the experiment will yield interesting data, it might make sense to take the risk without authorization—do an experiment to determine if there's value in the idea. Then you have data to share with those who need to approve a larger investment.

.　　.　　.

We embrace a culture of experimentation at STVP, where we explicitly define our center as a laboratory in which we do experiments related to entrepreneurship education. By viewing each new project as an experiment, we get lots of latitude when we try new things, and nobody is surprised if the results are other than those we anticipated. It also gives us the freedom to ramp up or terminate projects depending upon the results of our experiments.

For example, we did early experiments with podcasts (before they were called such) with great results, and scaled up this effort successfully. On the other hand, after offering a handful of massive open online courses (MOOCs), we decided that they were not worth the enormous effort and expense needed to deliver each one. Had we written up a detailed business plan and committed to these ideas before we started, *both* plans would have been works of fiction. There was no way to know what would happen until we performed the experiments.

Over the past few years, many companies have taken to hosting "hackathons" to formalize the process of experimentation. They bring teams together to tackle a specific challenge, or a challenge of each team's choosing, and spend a few hours or days focused on radical experimentation. Because the time commitment is short, there is little downside if a project doesn't work—yet there is a huge upside if it does. Once people hit upon an idea that shows some potential after initial experimentation, their motivation increases and the experimentation continues.

A great example of the layer-upon-layer experimentation that is needed to bring an idea to life comes from Anne Fletcher. She has been tackling the challenge of helping tiny seedlings stay alive. Like so many other gardeners, she learned from experience that seedlings die if they aren't kept moist. Anne's goal was to create a way to help them survive under circumstances where they aren't watered daily.

The goal of helping seedlings is easier said than done. Over the last two years, Anne has experimented with hundreds of designs, beginning with a new type of drip irrigation and ultimately designing seed pots with spots for six seeds, with a reservoir of water inside. The pots are made of clay, which is porous, so the water slowly leaches into the soil and keeps the seedlings moist. The pots need to be filled with water only weekly, not daily, to guarantee a steady dose of water.

Once she decided that these seed pots would work, Anne tried a long list of variables, keeping careful track of each experiment. Each pot she makes has a serial number so that she can track the results of every combination of variables over time. She experiments with different clay composition, thickness, and glazing, and with firing techniques. Anne knows from past experience that the path ahead is riddled with successes and failures. Each success opens the door to the next challenge—and the next series of failures. All of these experiments led Anne to found a company, called Orta, that manufactures the seed pots in their own factory in Redwood City, California, where the experimentation continues.

Many people would look at this story and say that the initial idea was "cheap," and that the value was added in the implementation. I completely disagree. As I have said many times, ideas aren't cheap at all—they are free. There is a big difference. When things are cheap, they don't have any value. When they are free, they are priceless. Ideas, such as seed pots to protect young seedlings, have great value. But it takes a significant commitment to bring these ideas to fruition. Each idea is like one of the seeds that Anne is helping to nurture. It might be small and vulnerable, but it has the potential to grow into a plant that bears fruit and generates the next generation of seeds. This is at the core of the Invention Cycle, in that ideas that are carefully tended ultimately lead to wave upon wave of fresh ideas.

Another example of the power of experimentation comes from Dr. Piya Sorcar, and her heroic efforts to prevent AIDS in the developing world. While a student in the Learning Sciences and Technology and Design Program at Stanford, Piya read reports about the dismal state of knowledge about AIDS in India. In 2006, when Piya started her work, it was estimated that nearly 6 million people in India were infected with HIV, and without proper education, those numbers would grow astoundingly fast.

Millions of dollars were being spent to educate people in India about AIDS transmission and treatment, but it was effectively ineffective. Surveys that Piya conducted in schools showed that despite the campaigns, there were grave misconceptions and a general lack of knowledge. Piya dove into the process of learning why this was the case so that she could develop new materials that would work.

After interviewing hundreds of people, it became clear that AIDS education couldn't be addressed in a one-size-fits-all way. Each region of the world has its own vocabulary, social taboos, and policies that needed to be taken into account. For example, in some regions of India the teachers literally burned the pamphlets that they were given to teach students about AIDS. They found the pictures much too explicit, and they didn't feel comfortable teaching the subject. Rather than distribute the material, they destroyed it. In fact, sex education had been banned in multiple states.

Piya took on the challenge of creating HIV educational materials that were highly tailored for the local cultures in India, that would achieve a high knowledge retention rate. With the drive to make a difference, Piya and a team of interdisciplinary researchers from Stanford experimented endlessly to test a wide array of approaches, from using stick figures to medical illustrations, and a wide variety of metaphors. After years of research and trial and error work, they developed a set of videos, with two-dimensional characters, that was both socially acceptable and easily comprehensible.

To ensure that all the material was accurate, they translated the material back and forth to make sure there were no mistakes. This led to some important insights and surprises. For example, in some local languages, the words for "treatment" and "cure" are the same, leading to the misconception that AIDS has a cure, when it doesn't.

The next step was to gain community acceptance of the materials from teachers, parents, and the government. Piya rallied support from high profile Indian celebrities, including actors and musicians, who lent their voices to the educational software. She experimented with every tool she could find to engage these key supporters, figuring out what motivated each of them. Some were swayed by the research, some by the poignant stories of success, and others by the list of other celebrities who participated.

Chapters 3 and 4 have shown that motivation and experimentation are deeply related. Creative problem solving depends upon your being motivated to address the problem, which in turn leads to experimentation in the quest for an effective solution. The results provide data, which then refuels your motivation. This is a feed-forward loop: your motivation leads to experimentation, which leads to more motivation and more experimentation. This is how tiny seeds of inspiration grow into big ideas.

## Projects

1. Practice making pretotypes. Pick a few challenges/ opportunities in your life—big or small—and design and perform different types of pretotypes to evaluate the feasibility of various solutions. Consider what approach you will use for each—the Mechanical Turk, the Pinocchio Technique, or the Facade. For example, how might you create a pretotype for a new item on a restaurant menu, a pillow with a built-in alarm clock, or an app that offers personalized exercise protocols?

2. Look at the list of things that motivate you from the prior chapter and design some experiments that would address these challenges/opportunities.

3. Do an experiment; try something you've never done before and see what happens. It can be a social, physical, or intellectual experiment. Actively evaluate the results of the experiment to extract what you've learned. Does this motivate you to do additional experiments in this area?

# Part Three

# Innovation

*Focus and Reframe*

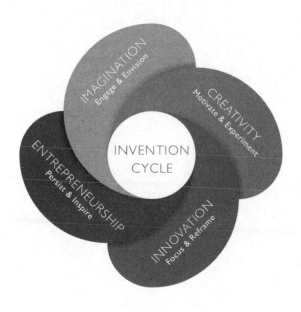

Envisioning the seashore is *imaginative.*

Painting a picture of the ocean is *creative.*

Developing a novel way to capture the beauty of the waves is *innovative.*

That is exactly what Katherine (Kay) Young has done: she moved from imagination to creativity to innovation as she perfected a unique method of capturing the majesty of the ocean. This requires great focus and the ability to look at a familiar technique with fresh eyes.

Kay grew up near the coast of Virginia, was drawn to the water, and took art classes so that she could learn how to paint pictures of ocean waves. She honed her technique so that she could flawlessly capture the movement of the water and the crashing of waves on the shore with oil paint. This was a hobby that Kay pursued in her free time while she went through college and medical school, and afterward as a plastic surgeon in San Francisco.

One day a few years ago, Kay was feeling restless with her artwork and wanted to take it to another level. While looking through some old art supplies Kay found some gold foil—actual gold that has been hammered to the thickness of tissue paper—that she had used years earlier to apply to furniture. Having enjoyed that process, she decided to play around with the gold foil. She found a small block of wood that she would normally use as the surface for a painting and covered it in the gold. Curious about what would happen, Kay then painted a seascape on top of the gold foil. The results were remarkable.

When Kay painted the ocean waves on the foil, using a thin coat of oil paint, a tiny amount of the metal showed through. Though she couldn't actually see the gold, the metal background significantly changed the way light bounced off the image, giving the scene a much greater range of light and dark than a traditional oil painting. Paired with Kay's ability to capture the scene in exquisite detail, the new background made the painting look as though you were viewing the ocean through a window, with natural light, instead of on a painted canvas.

For the past few years Kay has been experimenting with this technique, using gold and silver foil behind her paintings, to capture the moods of the ocean and the sky at different times of day with a wide range of weather. This approach resonates with Kay's goal of using ocean scenes to reflect upon our own lives. She calls this series of work "Places for Reflection."

Kay would never have developed this innovative technique without years of building her technical skills and challenging assumptions about what it means to capture scenes with oil paint. This is the key to innovation: build upon your imagination (engage and envision) and your creativity (self motivation and experimentation), to then innovate (focus and reframe) in order to develop unique ideas.

Below is a sample of Kay's painting, shown in black and white. It is a visible reminder that innovation results from focused dedication and the ability to look at old things in new ways.

The Invitation, by Katherine Young

Chapter 5

# Focus

## *Take Out the Trash*

A few weeks ago I flew into Newark Airport. On arrival, I jumped into a taxi to my hotel in downtown New York City. As usual, I started chatting with the driver. He was from Haiti, his first language was French, he had two young children, and he had worked as a taxi driver fourteen to sixteen hours a day, six days a week, for fifteen years. I also learned that he had to wait about three hours at the airport for each new ride, hoped to earn about fifty dollars from each of his three daily fares, and was barely making ends meet.

It turns out that cab drivers at the airport spend an average of *nine hours a day* in a makeshift break room, waiting for their next ride. They spend most of that time watching

TV. An easy calculation reveals that fifty hours a week in the break room, for fifteen years, is a total of almost forty thousand hours. Wow! What might have happened if he had used even some of this time to master a new skill, such as learning to write computer code or how to do magic tricks?

While this is certainly an extreme example, most of us let a lot of time slip through our fingers. Do the math: There are twenty-four hours in a day. If you sleep eight of those hours and spend five hours on personal needs such as eating and bathing, you're left with eleven hours each day. That's seventy-seven hours a week. If you spend fifty hours each week working, you're still left with twenty-seven hours each week, or over fourteen hundred hours a year. That's an awful lot of time to spend as you wish.

We all have the same twenty-four hours in the day. It's up to you how you spend those hours. I frequently remind myself that the president of the United States, a Nobel Prize winner, and an Olympic athlete all have the same twenty-four hours in a day I do. They've found ways to achieve their impressive goals in the same amount of time that I—and you—have to spend each day.

Returning to the taxi driver, I learned that he had earned a certificate in repairing heating, ventilation, and air-conditioning (HVAC) systems, but had decided not to take a job in this field because the entry-level salary was lower than that of a cab driver. He had given up the chance at a long-term career in which he could have earned seniority, autonomy, and a higher salary, for a short-term win. This is known as "precrastination," or the tendency to complete, or at least begin, tasks as soon as possible, knowing that extra effort would have created a better outcome. Essentially, it's picking low-hanging fruit, even when it leads to lower value in the long run.

Here is a short description of a study about precrastination, done at Pennsylvania State University:

> To test the human capacity to precrastinate, researchers David Rosenbaum, Lanyun Gong, and Cory Adam Potts led 27 college students to an alley where there were two yellow plastic buckets filled with pennies—one on either side. On one side, the bucket was closer to the participant, and on the other, it was closer to the other end of the alley. The participants were asked to pick up either the right or left bucket, whichever seemed easiest, and carry it to the end of the alley.
>
> To their surprise, most participants chose the bucket that was closer to them, but further from the finish line. That is, they chose to carry the bucket for longer. In the debrief later, many said some variation on, "I wanted to get the task done as soon as I could."

So many of us do this. We make choices that give us a short-term win at the expense of long-term success. When cleaning up the house, do you stuff items into a "junk drawer" as opposed to taking a bit more time to sort them and throw some things away? Or, when building a product, do you cut some corners to get the task done sooner? In the world of technology, this is called technical debt or design debt. The debt refers to work that eventually needs to get done for a job to be fully completed. Many firms are willing to take on this debt in order to get a product out sooner. They know, however, that if not "repaid," the debt continues accumulating, making the work even more challenging later.

It takes considerable effort and dedication to select a significant long-term objective and then focus on accomplishing it, without cutting corners. You might be motivated enough to perform some quick experiments to test your ideas, as described in the chapters on creativity. However, if you don't have sustained focus, the long-term results will never materialize. Whether it's making a movie, starting a company, or becoming a magician, actually accomplishing a goal takes much more than motivation and experimentation, which are necessary but not sufficient. For example, you might make a quick storyboard for a film, jot a business plan on the back of a napkin, or buy a magic kit. Those initial steps need to be followed by the next one, where you dedicate your attention to that objective. Though this seems obvious, most people don't do it.

The key to focusing is actively carving out time to do so. This is easy to say, but it takes significant effort, as you move your objectives from the background to the foreground, prioritizing them above other distractions. An issue that many people face is that they fill their time with commitments and then, once their day or week is full, can't imagine ways to add anything new. They're busy tackling the things they *need* to do, so they don't have time to do the things they *want* to accomplish.

Over the years, I have developed a metaphor that helps me add and subtract obligations so that I can focus on the things that are most important. I think of my life as a trash compactor, filled with all my commitments. When I start a new project, for instance, the responsibilities fill up the entire trash compactor. Then, as I gain experience with the requisite tasks, I compress the compactor, and the tasks take up less space. For example, the first time I organized a large conference, it took all my time to develop the program and to build a network of resources. The second time around, I already had the list of resources and knew what had worked before. Planning the second conference took much less effort, allowing me to take on other projects, in parallel. The more experienced I became, the less time each one took, and the more parallel projects I was able to take on.

Essentially, each time you take on a new commitment, it's added to your trash compactor. If it leverages skills and resources you already have, it takes up less space from the start. And each time you accomplish the task, the compactor compresses because you become more efficient each time around, leaving more room for new projects. As you gain more and more experience, your compactor continues to squeeze the contents, leaving more room for new challenges. Eventually, however, the trash compactor is completely full, and you can't add anything else. It's now time to take out the trash.

There are three ways to deal with the contents of a full trash compactor: First, you can throw some of the contents away. Second, you can hand over some of the contents to other people, and they will add that stuff to their compactor. Finally, you can choose to keep it in your compactor. Below are examples of how these options have worked for me:

For a dozen years I ran the conferences referenced above, called Roundtables on Entrepreneurship Education. At first there was one conference a year at Stanford, which took most of my time to manage for several months. After a few years of experience, it took much less time to run the conference, and we added an additional annual conference in Europe, then one in Asia, another one in Latin America, and finally one in the Middle East.

At that point I was at the limit of my ability to manage all those conferences, in addition to all my other commitments. After weighing my options, I hired someone to take responsibility for all of our international programs. This new person started her job with an empty trash compactor, which she filled with these conferences. After she gained experience, she was able to compress her compactor and thus add additional programs. This expanded the range of offerings well beyond what I could have done on my own.

I chose a different route when it came to running our Global Innovation Tournament. This project started as an exercise in my creativity class, then grew to a campus-wide competition, and finally an international tournament. At that point, the work involved in running the program took over our entire team's time for several weeks. Practically nothing else could happen when we were running the tournament. We had a decision to make: we had to either staff up to support the competition, or give up the program altogether. We decided to capture what we had learned, put together a detailed guide for others, and declare victory. It had been a great experiment, but we decided to remove it completely from our trash compactor. It was something we were now happy to let others take on if they wished.

Finally, there are things that, despite the time and effort, I choose to always keep in my trash compactor. These are core activities that I don't want to outsource or give up. For example, the classes I teach are always in my compactor, and each year they take the same amount of time and effort. Each year there is a new teaching team, and we add new projects and assignments. These items are anchor tenants in my trash compactor. In the future, I can always decide to hand them over to others, or to stop them altogether, but for now they are core commitments that I work around.

I find this metaphor helpful in that it reminds me to periodically take out the trash. There are always projects that can be delegated or eliminated. Delegating allows the project to thrive while freeing up my time for parallel tasks, and deleting allows me to focus my attention on new initiatives.

Besides being mindful of what you spend your time *doing,* it's important to be mindful of what you *think about.* For example, if you have a long commute, are you spending the time solving the problems you need to address that day, catching up with friends on the phone, listening to a book or podcast, or quietly meditating to clear your mind? The choice is up to you, but that decision should be made with intention. In essence, your mindshare is just as important as your time-share. Our brains are always chewing on something, and we each need to decide what that will be. You can spend your thoughts frivolously, or you can spend them reaching clearly defined objectives that will lead to a large return on that investment. In fact, your attention and your thoughts are your most valuable asset.

Your thoughts also influence your body, which in turn influences your mind. For example, if you are anxious, your heart naturally starts to beat faster. Your mind interprets this as stress, which leads to an even faster heartbeat. This feedforward loop can get out of control, leading to severe anxiety. Being able to manage and defuse the cycle is critical, since these symptoms are not just uncomfortable, but they get in the way of accomplishing your goals.

An example comes from Justin Rosenstein, described earlier, who learned early on that being a leader requires controlling not just your thoughts but also your state of mind. Here is a short excerpt from a talk he gave at Stanford:

The most important part of being a leader is managing your own psychology. . . . How many people in the room have experienced some sort of voice in your head that sounds like it's your voice, but it's telling you, you are doing things badly? There is a voice that is self-doubting and judging. And it's very easy to confuse this voice for yourself, especially because it speaks in your own voice, but it's not. It's sort of like having an annoying judgmental roommate living in your head. You'll notice this now that I point it out. . . . I've done a ton of meditation work and I still hear this voice. But the difference is that I now have a new relationship to it. I hear the voice, I say, Thank you, I appreciate that you are trying to be helpful. You can keep hanging out in my head, that's totally fine. Kick your feet up, make yourself comfortable, but that's not me and I make decisions from a different place. And so I continue to act in the face of fear, even when those things keep coming up and telling me, Oh, you are screwing this up.

This skill is often called mindfulness, which is defined as focused, intentional, and nonjudgmental attention on your sensations, thoughts, and emotions in the present moment. As Thích Nhãt Hạnh writes, "In mindfulness one is not only restful and happy, but alert and awake." In today's fast-paced, interconnected world, it takes extreme effort to focus mindfully. We are so often multitasking, with constant interruptions and distractions. Emails, text messages, phone calls, tempting social media updates, and the chatter of colleagues in open offices offer continuous diversions, breaking our focus. This has been shown to significantly reduce the quality and quantity of what we can achieve.

Tristan Harris, a software designer, has spent the past several years studying how we spend our time so that he can design products that help us manage it more wisely. In his TEDx talk in Brussels, he compared checking your email, news feeds, and/or social media updates repeatedly to playing a slot machine. Each time we refresh the screen to see if there's anything new, it's like gambling. Even though we play with small amounts of time—like small coins in a slot machine—it eventually adds up to a fortune. Without being mindful about how we use our time, this valuable resource slips through our fingers.

Ellen Langer, a social psychologist at Harvard, has been doing research on mindfulness for decades and has gained great insights into the power of focused attention on creativity and performance in general. Here is an excerpt from a recent interview with Ellen Langer in *Harvard Business Review*:

Mindfulness is the process of actively noticing new things. When you do that, it puts you in the present. It makes you more sensitive to context and perspective. It's the essence of engagement. . . . I've been studying this for nearly 40 years, and for almost any measure, we find that mindfulness generates a more positive result. . . . No matter what you're doing—eating a sandwich, doing an interview, working on some gizmo, writing a report—you're doing it mindfully or mindlessly. When it's the former, it leaves an imprint on what you do. At the very highest levels of any field—Fortune 50 CEOs, the most impressive artists and musicians, the top athletes, the best teachers and mechanics—you'll find mindful people, because that's the only way to get there.

Cliff Nass, formerly of Stanford's Communication Department, studied the consequences of attempting to pay attention to several things at the same time. He found that those who think they're good at multitasking typically are actually terrible at doing so. The more multitasking they do, the worse multitaskers perform. In addition, they don't notice the mistakes they are making.

Cliff Nass and his colleagues ran a study in which they showed self-identified multitaskers sets of two red rectangles alone or surrounded by two, four, or six blue rectangles. They flashed each configuration twice, and the subjects had to determine if the two red triangles in the second frame were in the same position as in the first frame. They were told not to pay attention to the surrounding blue triangles. Their scores were terrible compared to those who don't multitask frequently, an indication that frequent multitasking damages a person's ability to focus.

Focusing on one thing for a significant block of time leads to much greater productivity and creativity. According to Daniel Levitin, author of *The Organized Mind: Thinking Straight in the Age of Information Overload:*

> If you want to be more productive and creative, and to have more energy, the science dictates that you should partition your day into project periods. Your social networking should be done during a designated time, not as constant interruptions to your day. . . . Increasing creativity will happen naturally as we tame the multitasking and immerse ourselves in a single task for sustained periods of, say, 30 to 50 minutes.

Greg McKeown also writes about the importance of focus in his book *Essentialism: The Disciplined Pursuit of Less,* in which he points out that the word *focus* can be both a verb and a noun. This distinction is important, since success isn't just the *act* of focusing but also *selecting* the right thing on which to focus. He created a graphic that illustrates the value of giving your undivided attention, as well as attending to the things that matter most.

| | high | |
|---|---|---|
| **Get the wrong** thing done | | **Get the right** thing done |
| **Get almost nothing** done | | **Get a bit of everything** done |

FOCUS AS A NOUN (vertical axis, high to low)

low — high

FOCUS AS A VERB

Greg uses the examples of both Bill Gates and Warren Buffett, both of whom acknowledge that the key to their success is the ability to do both types of focus—noun and verb. They see themselves as "editors in chief," selecting the things that deserve focus. Greg writes:

> Focusing on what is essential is a powerful ability, perhaps the most powerful in a world where we are so bombarded with distracting ideas, information and opinions. However, if we want to consistently give our energies to what is essential we need to develop both kinds of focus. Only in this way can we answer with confidence the question, "What's important now?"

This resonates with the classic work of Stephen Covey, who wrote *The Seven Habits of Highly Successful People*. He argues that success comes from understanding the importance and urgency of everything we do. In his model, there are four categories of activities: urgent and important, urgent and unimportant, not urgent and important, and not urgent and not important. Covey argues that 90 percent of people spend most of their time on things that are *urgent* and *important,* and 10 percent of their time "vegging out" on *non-urgent* and *unimportant* activities. Others spend most of their time doing things that are *urgent* but *not important.* They think they are doing something useful, but are really just wasting time.

Covey says that effective people focus on activities that are *important,* even if they aren't urgent. Though it might seem counterintuitive, he urges people to spend most of their time on activities that are important but *not* urgent. This includes planning for the future and building relationships. This way, you prepare for the future and get all your work completed. Covey says that, if you did this, "your effectiveness would increase dramatically. Your crises and problems would shrink to manageable proportions because you would be thinking ahead, working on the roots."

There are several tactical things you can do to help you focus on the most important tasks. One is having a clean, clear workspace. When your space is a mess, the clutter puts a significant cognitive load on your brain. Researchers at Princeton and the University of Illinois have demonstrated, using functional magnetic resonance imaging (fMRI), that the more things there are fighting for your attention, the less able you are to focus, and the more stressed you become. Essentially, when our world is cluttered, so are our thoughts.

We can look to top chefs for inspiration. They have developed a process called *mise-en-place,* a French phrase that refers to the practice of gathering and arranging all necessary ingredients before they begin cooking. The practice, which eliminates unwanted distractions, results in both discipline and focus. For many chefs, this practice spills over into their lives outside the kitchen. They internalize the philosophy, making sure that they prioritize every minute and every resource even when they aren't cooking.

In addition to decluttering your workspace to improve focus, you can make sure that the mind occupying that workspace is sharp and recharged. Your skills are deeply compromised when you aren't rested. Research by William D. S. Killgore at Harvard Medical School reinforces prior work demonstrating that cognitive abilities in general are compromised by a lack of sleep. His work supports work by others showing that sleep deprivation leads to a slowing of thought processing, impairs memory, makes it difficult to learn, and lowers reaction times. In short, the work you do while awake is deeply influenced by the quality and quantity of sleep you are getting.

Focus turns your mind into a sharp knife that can cut to the core of a problem. This requires putting in both the timeshare and the mindshare to address something that is meaningful to you, taking out the trash to get rid of obligations that aren't important anymore, and keeping your mind and workspace clean so you can really focus.

## Projects

1. See how long you can focus on a project without interrupting yourself. Pick a quiet spot and a task you want to accomplish. If you find yourself easily distracted, look for ways to eliminate distractions, one by one. For example, close your computer, shut off your cell phone, and remove from your desk items that draw your attention.

2. What's in your trash compactor? What things might you delegate or eliminate?

3. Review the matrix designed by Greg McKeown on page 117. Are you not only focused on the right things, but also able to actively focus? If not, what do you need to do to get into the upper-right quadrant?

Chapter 6

# Reframe

## *Retrain Your Brain*

Twenty-two years ago my husband, Mike, and I separated for two years after seven years of marriage. During that impossibly difficult time, I had a revelation that changed the way I saw—and still see—everything.

During our separation, there were days when I felt particularly positive about my marriage and mentally listed dozens of things about my husband that made me optimistic about our future together. There were other days, however, when the idea of reconciliation seemed impossible as I clicked off all the ways in which we were incompatible.

One day I stepped back to examine these mental lists and, to my surprise, discovered that many of the things I appreciated about my marriage were the *same* ones that frustrated me. That insight opened my eyes to the idea that I was painting the picture of our marriage in my mind, and that I could change that image by shifting the frame I was using. The frame that focused on the positive interpretations, as opposed to the negative interpretations, provided a path to repairing our marriage. Now, over twenty years later (and having just celebrated our twenty-ninth anniversary), Mike and I are incredibly appreciative that we made it through that challenging time.

The power to change your frame of reference is relevant far beyond marriage. Applicable to creative problem solving in all parts of life, it's one of the keys to innovation. The perspectives, or frames, we use are influenced by past experiences, current circumstances, and our state of mind. By understanding this, we can actively shift those frames to reveal important insights. Of course, some of our frames are nailed down pretty tightly and are hard to shift. But even those can be moved with effort. We can reframe things as small as a computer password and as large as a career.

In 2011, designer Mauricio Estrella was in a particularly bad state of mind, reeling from the painful breakup of his marriage. As a result, he was not thrilled when his computer stopped working, as it did with frustrating regularity, demanding that he change his password. This tiny request was just one more annoyance in his day. Mauricio writes that in that moment he actively chose to look at his computer password differently. Below is a condensed version of his story:

Letting all the frustration go, I remembered a tip I heard from my former boss, Rasmus. Somehow he combined to-do lists with passwords, and I thought to use an augmented variation of that.

I'm gonna use a password to change my life . . .

My password became the indicator. My password reminded me that I shouldn't let myself be a victim of my recent breakup, and that I'm strong enough to do something about it.

My password became: "Forgive@h3r"

During the rest of the week, I had to type this password several times a day. . . .

In my mind, I was reminding myself to "Forgive her." That simple action changed the way I looked at my ex-wife. That constant reminder that I should forgive her led me to accept the way things happened at the end of my marriage, and embrace a new way of dealing with the depression that I was drowning in.

In the following days, my mood improved drastically. By the end of the 2nd week, I noticed that this password became less powerful, and it started to lose its effect. A quick refresh of this "mantra" helped me. I thought to myself *I forgive her* as I typed it, every time. The healing effect of it came back almost immediately. . . .

One month later, my dear exchange server asked me again to renew my password. I thought about the next thing I had to get done.

My password became Quit@smoking4ever

And guess what happened. I'm not kidding you. I quit smoking overnight.

One month later, my password became Save4trip@ thailand

Guess where I went 3 months later. Thailand!

As described by Ian Urbina in the *New York Times,* others have used passwords as a way to motivate them to win a race, remember an important date, or hide a secret. This is a useful reminder that something as small as a password can be used to practice reframing.

Even when we don't actively choose a frame of reference, one is always there. For instance, when we listen to music lyrics and don't fully understand what they're saying, we fill in the gaps with what we think they are, based on our own frame. This even has a name—it's called a mondegreen, as described by Alina Simone on Public Radio International:

The word mondegreen was coined in an essay by writer Sylvia Wright in which she described misinterpreting a line from the Scottish ballad "The Bonnie Earl of Moray." The actual line was, "They have slain the Earl o' Moray, and laid him on the green."

What did she hear? "They have slain the Earl o' Moray, and Lady Mondegreen."

It turns out there are scientific reasons for why it's so easy to misinterpret songs and poems. The first thing you have to understand is that "when we understand what someone says, it's always at least partly a hallucination," says Mark Liberman, a linguist at the University of Pennsylvania. Extracting meaning from sound actually depends on a combination of hearing and hoping. "There's a piece of what we understand that comes from the sound that comes in our ear," Liberman explains, but "there's a piece of what we understand that comes from the expectations in our brain."

Every day we interpret what others are doing by putting a frame around their actions. And we are often wrong. I distinctly remember a situation several years ago when I was at a meeting with some alumni. A young man in the group repeatedly checked his phone and sent text messages. I thought his behavior was rude, and in my mind I chastised him. At the end of the meeting, he apologized to me for his inattention; his infant son was in the hospital, he said, and he had been getting updates from his wife. I realized that I had made an assumption that was completely incorrect. Considered through my new frame, he was no longer rude but incredibly dedicated to have showed up at the meeting at all, given the circumstances.

So how does this relate to innovation? It is critical to understand that our frame of reference determines how we see the challenges and opportunities we face, and the type of ideas we generate. By shifting our frame, we unlock a wealth of fresh ideas. The more radically we shift the frame, the more unique the ideas we generate. Reframing is thus a powerful tool for identifying opportunities.

Perhaps you've heard the expression "A crisis is a terrible thing to waste." Credited to the economist Paul Romer, this saying reminds us that reframing allows us to see bigger problems as bigger opportunities. An example hits close to home for me. During the financial crisis in 2008, those of us in academia worried that the funds for our programs would evaporate. The Stanford Technology Ventures Program was at great risk; it was likely that many of those who donated to our center wouldn't be able to continue supporting our efforts. We used this as a chance to rethink our entire strategy for funding our program. We looked outside our normal base of support in Silicon Valley for backing—in fact, we decided to expand our focus to include the entire world. This allowed us to pursue partnerships in other countries, from Finland to Chile, which ultimately added depth to our offerings, provided exciting new opportunities for our faculty and students, and generated the revenue we needed to make it through the economic downturn. The crisis really was an opening for opportunities. Had we not been forced to question the status quo, we likely would never have explored these opportunities.

In a recent STVP class, one of our Mayfield Fellows presented a case study about how companies of all types deal with crises, and how some turn them into opportunities. Examples included Tylenol's response to tampering with their medication, Perrier's response to claims of benzene in their sparkling water, and Mercedes's response to their new car's failure of the "moose test" in Sweden. Clearly, some firms try to put Band-Aids on a crisis, while others use an unfortunate situation as an opportunity to actually strengthen trust by responding with bold initiatives that make them even stronger than before the incident.

The iconic example is Tylenol, which in 1982 suffered a blow that could easily have destroyed the company. Their response has become a model for other firms. For reasons unknown, someone had replaced capsules of the pain medication with capsules of cyanide, resulting in seven deaths. The chairman of the parent company, Johnson & Johnson, made the decision to immediately withdraw all Tylenol from store shelves, demonstrating that the company would do anything to protect customers. Corporate leaders set up a hotline for consumers, held press conferences to communicate all that they knew, and announced new tamper-proof packaging with a glued box, a plastic seal over the neck of the bottle, and a foil seal over the mouth of the bottle. The new packaging was released only six months after the crisis, demonstrating how quickly the company was responding. All of these actions ultimately strengthened Johnson & Johnson's brand, even though they were triggered by a crisis.

Of course, nobody welcomes such a crisis. But when crises arise—as they are sure to do—they provide a powerful opportunity to rethink everything, to reframe the way you approach the world, and to stretch your perspective in ways you might not have known you could.

We each have tremendous capacity for flexibility in our thinking, which is why we have so much potential for innovation. This flexibility can literally be seen in the brain, on both microscopic and anatomic levels. On the microscopic level, researchers can see tiny spines on neurons form and disappear in response to different inputs. On the anatomic level, scientists can see entire portions of the brain change functionally as a result of changing behavior. This phenomenon is called homuncular flexibility.

*Homunculus,* Latin for "little man," is used in modern science to describe the distorted scale model of the body that maps to the sensory and motor areas of our brains. The model is distorted because much more space in the human brain's cortex is dedicated to sensory input from, and motor output to, certain parts of the body, including the hands, mouth, and eyes, while much less space is dedicated to the arms and legs. Below is a picture of a sample homunculus, showing how our brain actually sees our body.

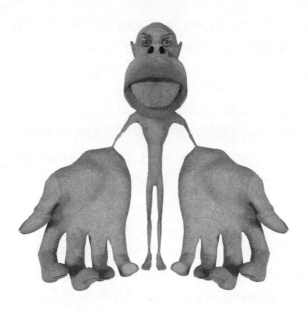

Homuncular flexibility occurs because the brain is "plastic." That is, it changes in response to how it is used. If someone loses his or her vision, for example, the part of the brain responsible for processing visual information shrinks and the part that processes sound increases. Similarly, when someone plays the piano or violin, the part of the brain that controls the fingers grows significantly larger. These changes occur because the brain is able to respond to the changing demands of the body. This process is particularly relevant to innovation because it demonstrates that we are capable of physically changing the way we think.

This can be demonstrated using virtual reality (VR). In VR, you put on goggles and earphones that fill your eyes and ears with a fantasy world, and you are connected to a

computer via sensors on your body. With the help of sophisticated software, your sensory inputs change based on
your movements, allowing you to interact with the virtual
world. At Stanford's Virtual Human Interaction Laboratory
(VHIL), run by Jeremy Bailenson, they've developed VR
experiences that allow you to fly through a city like Superman, swim with dolphins, watch yourself grow old, or even
become a coral reef that is threatened with ocean acidifica-
tion. Their research focuses on how these virtual experiences
change the way people think, learn, and act.

Virtual reality can also allow you to control a virtual tail
or an extra arm. After only a short time, your brain adjusts to
control these brand-new appendages. Researchers at University College London gave thirty-two volunteers a virtual tail
that they could control by moving their hips. The volunteers
then played a VR game in which they needed to use that tail
to hit colored lights that were out of reach of their onscreen
alter egos' hands. No one was told how to control the tail,
but they all learned quickly with experimentation. In just ten
minutes, the volunteers could control the tail as easily as they
could their hands.

With a background in neuroscience and a passion for
teaching creativity and innovation, I decided to partner with
the VHIL lab to bring this technology into the classroom in
a new course, called Engineering Innovation. My goal was to
use this tool to provide students with experiences that challenge their assumptions about what is possible in the real
world. My hope was that the experience would spill over into

their "real" lives, encouraging them to challenge assumptions and reframe problems more readily.

In the class, we were fortunate to have access to several Oculus Rift headsets that we used along with headphones to create virtual experiences. The students took turns using the technology that allowed them to enter a completely different world. In one case, the students experienced the world through the eyes of a cartoonlike elephant with a long, swinging trunk. In this scenario, they moved forward through a fanciful, virtual amusement park filled with enormous objects that appeared to be made out of foam rubber. The students quickly learned how to control their new trunk by moving their head up, down, and sideways. By swinging their trunk, they could knock over buildings, bat huge balls into the air, and topple over cartoon cars.

After participating in this experience, the students did a "real world" exercise that required them to look at old things in new ways, such as figuring out how travelers can have the things they need at their destination without carrying a suitcase. Although this wasn't a controlled experiment, the students in the class claimed that the virtual reality activity primed them to see the world through different lenses and made them much more comfortable looking at the classroom challenge with a fresh perspective. Their ideas included drones that follow you around the airport, 3-D printers that create whatever a traveler needs on the spot, a service that rents clothes at the destination, a standard uniform that *everyone* wears so that no one needs to take a change of clothes, and (my favorite) a suitcase that travels around the world independent of its owner; when the traveler arrives at the destination, the suitcase, full of clean clothes, automagically finds its way to its owner.

There are many ways to reframe the way you see the world without using virtual reality goggles. One approach is to actively examine your assumptions and then question them. By digging deep and uncovering those assumptions, you're then able to start challenging them. I routinely run an exercise with students and executives in which I give teams a list of industries, from airlines to zoos, and ask them to list all their assumptions about one of those industries. Then I ask them to turn those assumptions upside down, imagining what would happen if the opposite were true. For example, here are a few of the assumptions one team generated for hotels:

- Room keys
- Little soaps
- Tourists
- Room service
- Noisy hallways
- Far from home
- Pillow chocolate

- Mini-bar with key
- Check-out time
- Concierge
- TV in room
- Housekeeping
- Expensive food
- Wake-up calls

Each of these assumptions opens the door for a challenge. For example, what would have to happen for a hotel to offer flexible check-in and check-out times? What would it be like if local hosts, rather than a hotel concierge, helped guests find their way around? What if there were an open kitchen where you could make yourself a snack at any time of the day or night? What if you could select a specific room, as you do an airplane seat? What if hotels were designed not for out-of-town guests, but for local getaways with friends and family? The students used their list of assumptions to generate several brand-new concepts for hotels by turning some of the expectations on their head.

Another team worked on rethinking movie theaters. After unpacking their assumptions and challenging them, they came up with several very interesting ideas, including a new movie concept called Move Ease, which would combine a bicycle spin class with a movie theater. Instead of sitting still, patrons would exercise while watching the movie. In their pitch, the team suggested that patrons pay at the end of the film—the more exercise people did, the lower the price of the experience, encouraging them to get a harder workout.

Another way to reframe a problem is to come up with the stupidest solutions you can think of. As discussed in detail in *What I Wish I Knew When I Was 20*, dumb ideas help surface your assumptions by tapping into your core beliefs about what can't be done. For example, it might seem absurd to suggest having candy for breakfast, wearing the same clothes each day, or hitchhiking to work. But these suggestions lead to interesting new breakfast, fashion, and commuting ideas.

I recently asked a group of students to come up with a challenge in their lives—something that seemed impossible. This group collectively decided that they wanted to travel around the world but didn't have any money. Traveling extensively for free seemed like an insurmountable problem. I then asked them to brainstorm to come up with the *worst* ideas they could for addressing this challenge. One of their many ideas was to get a private jet on layaway, so that they wouldn't have to pay for it until later. That seemed like a pretty silly idea, quite unreasonable.

I then asked them to brainstorm *again* to figure out how they might make that actually happen. Lo and behold, within a few minutes they had found a way that just might work. They decided to create a reality TV show in which a group of twenty-year-old students travel around the world starting businesses in different countries. Each week the program would showcase a different destination and a new venture designed to meet the needs of that local community. Viewers would get to see different areas of the world, learn about the local business environment, and watch how these young people attempted to launch a new business at each destination. To make this happen, they would find corporate sponsors at each destination.

Once they looked at the challenge that way, the possibility of traveling around the world without a fortune to invest wasn't so far-fetched. Although they didn't pursue the idea, the students realized that looking at their problem from a new perspective had allowed fresh ideas to emerge. This type of reframing is another key to innovation.

Let's see how this plays out in an entrepreneurial venture: Tristan Walker, CEO of Walker and Company, parlayed a personally difficult situation into a new company. Tristan grew up in the projects of New York City. Committed to making a better life for himself, he worked doggedly in school, making sure that he was always at the top of his class. His teachers and mentors noticed his dedication and provided Tristan with opportunities to get experience and a better education. He went to Stony Brook University, where he was the valedictorian, and then headed to Wall Street.

When he was nineteen years old, Tristan had a summer internship in finance at Lehman Brothers. The first day of work, he took a tour of the stock-trading floor, along with one hundred other interns. As he walked into the room, a trader shouted at Tristan, "Get that shit off your face."

He went home to contemplate his dilemma. As a black man, he had a big problem with shaving his curly facial hair and, therefore, often had a day or two's beard growth. This problem was not unique to him. Today's razors have several blades, and they're designed to pull the facial hair up and actually cut the hair *below* the skin, resulting in a very close and smooth shave. For men with coarse, curly hair, this is a problem. The hair is cut below the skin, as intended—but when it grows back, it doesn't grow straight, but curly. The result is hair poking into the skin from beneath, leading to bumps and discomfort. For a self-conscience young man, this wasn't just uncomfortable, but painfully embarrassing.

Tristan went to the drugstore to see if he could find a shaving solution. The only options clearly made for black men were buried on the bottom shelf and covered in dust. The photo on the box was of an old black man, and it wasn't clear how the product was to be used. It didn't appear that this product was for him, either. So Tristan purchased a multi-blade razor, which took care of the beard but left him with the inevitable irritated bumps all over his face.

This dilemma stuck with Tristan as he moved through his career, leaving Wall Street for Stanford Business School, Twitter, Foursquare, and then, as an entrepreneur in residence, Andreessen Horowitz. His goal as an entrepreneur in residence was to identify a new business to launch. Ten years after his embarrassing encounter on the trading floor, he decided to reframe the dilemma that had vexed him for years. Instead of looking at his challenging facial hair as a problem, how could it be opened up as an opportunity? This new perspective led to his latest venture.

Tristan launched Walker and Company with the goal of making health and beauty easier for people of color. With intense focus, Tristan and his team took on the challenge with fresh eyes, creating an entire shaving system, including shaving brushes, blades, and lotions, as well as educational materials that show how and why they're used. Tristan's venture was launched a decade after he initially encountered the problem. This is not unusual. It often requires years of preparation and incubation to set the stage for reframing a problem to find an effective solution.

Each situation in our lives can be viewed with different frames. A wonderful short story told by Benjamin Zander and Rosamund Stone Zander in their book, *The Art of Possibility,* sums this up: A shoe factory sends two marketing scouts to a region of Africa to study the prospects for expanding business. The first scout sends a telegram back to the factory, saying, "Situation hopeless. No one wears shoes." But the second sends the triumphant message, "Glorious business opportunity. They have no shoes."

We each experience the world with a set of assumptions that are derived from our past experiences and current state of mind. By questioning those assumptions, seeing challenges as opportunities, and being willing to shift our perspective, we can unlock innovative ideas that are new in the world.

We've now traveled the path of the Invention Cycle from imagination, to creativity, to innovation. Along the way, we've explored how one's attitudes (envisioning, motivation, and focus) and actions (engage, experiment, and reframe) unfold, revealing opportunities, insights, and fresh ideas. Each stage builds upon the one before, creating sturdy scaffolding that can be scaled time and time again. We now move on to entrepreneurship, where we apply these skills, bringing our ideas to fruition.

## Projects

1. Practice homuncular flexibility by learning to write or brush your teeth with your nondominant hand.

2. Pick something in your everyday life that you don't enjoy, and find a way to make it enjoyable. Think of ways that you could look at the situation differently and specific things you could do to change the experience.

3. Look at the goals you have for yourself and come up with a list of crazy ways in which you could accomplish them. Figure out how you might make those ideas work in reality.

Part Four

# Entrepreneurship

*Persist and Inspire*

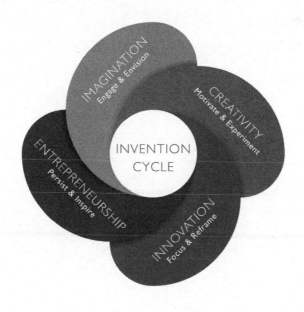

Several years ago, I was working with colleagues at the Universidad del Desarrollo and Universidad Católica in Chile. We were crafting ways to ramp up entrepreneurship education at both schools, and in the country as a whole, and challenged ourselves to come up with something so bold that it would light a huge fire of enthusiasm.

As part of our brainstorming, we came up with a big idea. What if we hired a ship—an "entrepreneur ship"—and took students from the two Chilean universities and Stanford to Patagonia in the south of Chile? The ship would travel for five days, with daily port calls, through magnificent fjords, with vistas of mountains, glaciers, and wildlife, allowing the students to experience the amazing beauty of the region, build cultural bridges, learn design thinking tools, and take on local entrepreneurial challenges. We'd take along a photographer and a videographer to capture the story so that we could share it.

Great idea, right? So what happened next?

We started pitching the idea to university administrators, companies in Chile that operate ships in Patagonia, groups that might have local challenges for the students to take on, organizations that might be amenable to funding the effort, reporters we wanted to cover the story, and students in both Chile and California.

The effort took several years, as we built support for the initiative, raised funds, gathered potential projects for the students, and put all the logistics in place. Finally it was time to select the students. At Stanford we invited those who were interested to gather for a group "interview." We set up a large tub of water with a fan at one end, simulating the fierce winds of Patagonia. Teams of students had to build a boat in ten minutes out of materials on hand, such as aluminum foil, rubber bands, and tape. The ship had to navigate from one end of the tub to the other while carrying a load of pennies. This short exercise quickly revealed the best team players as well as those who were eager to dive right in.

In March 2013, over Stanford's spring break, twenty Stanford students, forty Chilean students, and a dozen faculty members from Stanford, Universidad del Desarrollo, and Universidad Católica set sail. Each day there were lectures and workshops on creative problem solving, sessions about the local environment, and shore excursions to experience Patagonia. Together, on cross-cultural teams, the students tackled challenges such as how to improve a local town economy, promote ecotourism in Patagonia, improve primary school education in the region, and build more bridges between Chile and California. It was remarkable to see this idea finally come to life!

# Entrepreneurship

This was an entrepreneurial undertaking—an act of creation: going from nothing to something. It was built on the premise that you can accomplish much more than is imaginable with much less than seems possible. This process requires deep-seated persistence and the ability to mobilize others, both of which are discussed in the following chapters.

# Chapter 7

# Persist

## *What Floats Your Boat?*

Wearing nothing but a Speedo bathing suit, goggles, and a swim cap, Lewis Pugh was the first person to complete a long-distance swim in every ocean of the world, including the Arctic Ocean at the North Pole, where he swam for eighteen minutes in the frigid water. Lewis took on this incredible feat, driven by his motivation to bring awareness about the impact of climate change on the most vulnerable ecosystems in the world. He chose the North Pole to vividly demonstrate that this region, which should be covered in ice, has already melted.

Lewis imagined the activity many hundreds of times during his year-long training. This visualization allowed him to see the entire process, from start to finish, in his mind's eye. He built a team of twenty-nine people from ten countries to help him accomplish his goal, including a doctor, a navigator, and several trainers. Together they came up with a set of innovations that allowed him to succeed, including new exercise protocols and recovery procedures that allowed Lewis to take on this remarkable challenge.

Lewis was born in Plymouth, England, and as a child he saw the statues of famous explorers who had set off from Plymouth, including Sir Francis Drake, who carried out the second circumnavigation of the world in the 1500s. Lewis decided at the age of seven that he, too, would do something remarkable. When he was ten years old, Lewis's family moved to Cape Town, South Africa, where again the ocean surrounded him. He trained to become a maritime lawyer with the hope of protecting the seas, but soon discovered that this was not enough for him. Lewis wanted to have a much bigger impact. In 2003, he came up with the bold idea that he would swim all the endangered bodies of water in the world to bring awareness to environments in need of protection.

After a year of planning and preparation, Lewis was ready. His entire team hitched a ride on a cargo ship to the North Pole and asked the captain to stop briefly so that they could complete their mission. The ocean water at that spot was 4,200 meters deep, and it was well below freezing; in addition, the team needed polar bear guards to ensure that Lewis wasn't attacked while in the water.

When Lewis dove into the frigid, pitch-black water, it literally took his breath away, and his hands felt like they were on fire. To make the task less daunting, he broke it into pieces in his mind. The team had planted flags of all the participating team members along the shore, and his teammates ran alongside him with signs giving him vital data about how far he had progressed. Lewis set his goal to swim past the first flag, then the second, the third, and so forth. Each flag was a reminder of someone who was as committed as he was to this mission. He couldn't let any of his teammates down.

When Lewis emerged from the water after the one-kilometer swim, his team pulled him into a small boat, wrapped him in a towel, and rushed him back to the ship for a warm shower. He literally needed to be thawed out. The water inside his fingers had frozen solid, and they were so swollen that they cracked open. He wouldn't have feeling in his fingers again for four months.

Lewis was able to accomplish this great feat with powerful persistence, which has since inspired hundreds of thousands of people around the world. His Arctic swim was both a mental and a physical feat. The task required incredible focus and courage, as well as countless hours of training to develop the necessary skills and strength.

Innovative endeavors of all types are literally willed into being with steadfast dedication. Consider the process of building a skyscraper or running a marathon. At the beginning there is nothing but the vision of accomplishing your goal. The stronger your drive to reach the finish line, the more tenacious you'll be and the more likely you are to reach your objective.

.   .   .

As with any skill, starting with small steps, you can practice building your mental stamina. I do this in my classes by giving students challenges that require them to stretch in ways they haven't tried before. For example, I often require them to come up with at least one hundred solutions to a given problem. The problem might be something silly, such as finding uses for rubber bands; or it might be more serious, such as how to save water during the drought. At first the thought of generating one hundred ideas strikes them as crazy, but once they mentally set this goal for themselves, they find it much easier to reach it.

In the spring of 2014, I taught an online course called Creativity: Music to My Ears, in partnership with Warner Bros. Records. All the course projects had a music theme. For example, the twenty-five thousand students who were participating were asked to introduce themselves by designing the album cover of their life. They also submitted a "mind map" that illustrated their audio observations of a nearby environment. The final project involved capturing lessons from the course using their own song lyrics.

A two-week team project in the course focused on using music to address a challenge. Students formed their own teams of up to seven people, using the team formation tools available on the NovoEd platform we used. Some teams had participants from several different continents, each bringing a different perspective. Together, each team selected a problem to tackle, such as a snoring sleeping partner or saving energy at home. The first task was to generate at least one hundred solutions to that problem, and all the solutions needed to involve music in some way. For many participants, a hundred ideas sounded ridiculous. In fact, some thought this must have been a typo. Several wrote on the class blog, "Tina must have meant ten ideas; . . . one hundred ideas is just too hard!"

"That's the point," I responded. "Innovation is hard work. It takes persistence to generate unique ideas." Once they understood that the process was supposed to be hard, most teams buckled down, pushed through the pain, and came up with the required number of solutions to the problem they'd chosen.

The students discovered that the most interesting ideas often bubbled up after they thought all possibilities had been exhausted. For example, after pushing through obvious solutions, such as playing music to drown out the snoring, one team came up with the idea for a face mask that translates loud snoring into calming music. And the team working on saving energy at home came up with the idea for a house that plays music that reflects the energy usage. When the house is "happy," with low energy consumption, the music in the background communicates this without residents' having to look at computer monitors. When the house is "unhappy" the music reflects this, too.

As inspiration, the course included video interviews with Warner Bros. musicians, including Josh Groban, Jason Mraz,

Lily Allen, and Mike Shinoda of Linkin Park. A unifying theme in their comments was how hard these artists work, both during the creative process and in bringing their songs to their fans. A tiny fraction of their songs are born fully formed. Most take months to craft; the artists and their colleagues endlessly rewrite the music and the lyrics.

As Josh Groban said, "A good day is when you go in and walk out hearing what you wanted to hear. A great day is when you walk out hearing what you never knew you wanted." He acknowledged that this happens only after hours of focused effort during which the creative team pushes past barriers to come up with something really innovative. He also described his life while on tour, which involves designing the days carefully to make sure he optimizes every two-hour performance.

I assign a similar team project to my students at Stanford, requiring them to push much further than they think they can. Once teams spend three weeks generating hundreds of ideas, selecting their favorites, building prototypes, and testing them with users to get feedback, they present their findings to the class. Afterward, I tell them that they will now start the project all over again.

The looks on the students' faces say it all. They're both shocked and frustrated. The directive to go back to the beginning seems like a punishment. Their frustration melts into acceptance, however, when they realize that this new assignment is actually an opportunity. The first time through revealed the first wave of solutions, and testing provided useful feedback. Going back to the beginning gives them a chance to do a better job. They dive back into their projects, and two weeks later their ideas and presentations are vastly improved.

By the end of the second round of work, the students' acceptance transforms into appreciation. Deep down they knew that they hadn't pushed far enough the first time, and that there was much room for improvement in their ideas, prototypes, and presentations. By the end of the course, many of the students rate this as one of their favorite assignments. They report that they've learned the importance of pushing past the point when they thought they were done, in order to persist and deliver their best work. If the course were longer, I could give the same assignment again and again and again. Each repetition would reveal a new wave of ideas and insights, and even better results.

The ability to push past the point when others stop is often referred to as "grit." It is the tendency to sustain interest in and effort toward a long-term goal. Much work has been done on the importance of personal grit on success in all domains. In fact, it has been found that grit is a much bigger predictor of success than is raw intelligence. Psychologist Angela Duckworth focuses her research on the impact of this trait on success. She writes:

[G]rit predicts surviving the arduous first summer of training at West Point and reaching the final rounds of the National Spelling Bee, retention in the U.S. Special Forces, retention and performance among novice teachers, and graduation from Chicago public high schools, over and beyond domain-relevant talent measures such as IQ, SAT or standardized achievement test scores, and physical fitness.

Duckworth created a Grit Scale, based on a dozen questions that measure perseverance. The questions focus on traits such as the ability to set goals, focus on a task for an extended period of time, and overcome setbacks along the way. She has found that these traits can change over the course of a lifetime, and that people can learn to have more grit. Duckworth and her colleagues have also found that grit is strengthened when people are taught that frustration and mistakes are a natural part of the learning process, not signs that you should give up. When I told the students in my class that it was *supposed* to be challenging to generate one hundred solutions to a problem, they were much more likely to succeed. This simple statement helped build their grit.

Grit is also a huge predictor of entrepreneurial success. Bringing a bold new idea to life exposes endless near-death experiences for the idea, and only those innovators with long-term dedication are able to thrive under such circumstances. Every new venture is essentially trying to die, and it takes a huge effort to keep it alive during its early days. A key aspect of grit is the ability to strive toward a long-term goal. You need a vision for the future (discussed in detail in the chapter on envisioning). You need the drive to attain that goal (as outlined in the chapter on motivation). And you need to focus your time and attention on reaching that goal (as described in the chapter on focus).

Over the years I have seen a pattern among those who successfully navigate the path from innovation to entrepreneurship. They know how to take steps that are large enough to be challenging, but small enough that they lead manageably toward the objectives. The more experienced the entrepreneur, the greater the size of the steps, and the more they accomplish. Leveraging what they've learned, the resources they've accumulated, and the confidence they've attained, successful entrepreneurs allow their goals to expand to meet their abilities.

Those who don't pace themselves properly are doomed to one of two fates: They take tiny steps that are low risk, but that don't take them very far. Or they take huge steps that are beyond their ability, and they inevitably stumble. The key is to find the step size that is right for you, with enough of a challenge to make it interesting, but not so much that you end up so bruised and broken that you aren't able to get up and try again.

Persistence comes in many forms, including hard work, dedication, and the ability to stand by your ideas when in the face of doubters. Many fabulous ideas sound crazy when they are first described, and it can be hard for others to embrace them. Examples include Tesla (a new car company—really?), Twitter (140-character messages—you have to be kidding), and SpaceX (that will never work!).

I often see people struggle to pursue their ideas, fearing that others, including their parents, won't approve. I remind those who ask for my advice that resistance to your ideas is actually a gift, in that it gives you a chance to test the strength of your own convictions. If you aren't willing to fight for your ideas at the beginning, you won't be able to fight for them when the challenges get more intense. If everyone always agreed with your ideas, you'd never know how strongly you believed in them, and you'd never know if you were pursuing them for yourself or someone else. Universal approval also suggests that you probably aren't stretching far enough or seeking out objective critics.

Those who have achieved significant accomplishments have all faced people who opposed their ideas, and yet they had the ability to stay steadfast in their goals. Looking at them after they have reached a certain level of success, we don't often see their dedication in the face of early criticism. It's helpful to look at their entire path, to see how they started, the initial steps they took, and how each accomplishment built upon the one before. The stepping stones get larger and farther apart, but it's a path nonetheless, with many obstacles along the way.

Richard Branson provides a compelling example, As founder of Virgin Group, which holds more than four hundred companies, Branson began his entrepreneurial career with small endeavors; and with each success he stretched himself further. Branson started with a student magazine, then added a mail-order record business. After that, he opened a record store, which he grew into a chain of stores called Virgin Records. He picked the name Virgin because he and his small team were new to business. Following his success in retail, he launched a record label, also called Virgin Records. He continued adding one business after another—an airline, a game preserve, and a mobile phone company—building on his experience, resources, and confidence. As he says in his autobiography, "My interest in life comes from setting myself huge, apparently unachievable challenges and trying to rise above them. . . . [F]rom the perspective of wanting to live life to the full, I felt that I had to attempt it." His journey has been littered with failures, however, including those described below by a recent article in NextUp Asia:

> Virgin Cola, introduced by Richard Branson in 1994 as the rival to Coca-Cola, has practically disappeared. Virgin Clothes, launched on the stock exchange in 1996, folded with losses to shareholders, after debuting with promising new trends in providing more edgy wardrobe to the young. Virgin Money was launched with a viral and somewhat controversial advertising campaign, panned by critics with Richard Branson

emerging naked from the sea, but did not deliver the expected big financial rewards to its shareholders. Then came Virgin Vie, Virgin Vision, Virgin Vodka, Virgin Wine, Virgin Jeans, Virgin Brides, Virgin Cosmetics and Virgin Cars.

Branson says, "The challenge is to follow through on a great idea. If you've got a great idea, you need to just give it a try. And if you fall flat on your face, pick yourself up and try again. Learn from your mistakes. And, remember, you've got to go make a real difference in people's lives if you're going to be successful."

The quest to do something remarkable mandates leveraging the resources around you. But what are they? The first resource most people consider is money. Yes, that is necessary, but it is far from sufficient. In my classes, I have my students list all the resources they have, and to share that information with the class. It soon becomes clear that we have a great deal that we don't consciously value. For example, consider the Internet, a working car, a cell phone, friends and family, and good health. This is the tip of the iceberg. We all have *many* resources that we can leverage to accomplish our goals.

Even in the poorest parts of the world, there are resources. Consider refugees in Uganda who have practically nothing. Mohammed Osman Ali, a thirty-two-year-old Somali refugee, started a business by cobbling together parts for a video-game player and powering it with a diesel generator. He rents out time on this makeshift arcade to other refugees in ten-minute blocks. After escaping the war in Somalia in the back of a truck five years ago, after most of his family members were killed, Ali started the arcade and used the profits to open an adjoining store, which his wife manages; the store sells supplies such as paint, nails, and clothing. His success comes from leveraging the resources around him, though they are meager by any standards.

Keep in mind that there is a flip side to persistence. We can push ourselves so hard that we harm ourselves physically or mentally. I've experienced this. Here is my story:

I am incredibly fortunate to have a stimulating job, wonderful colleagues, and inspiring students. The possibilities in this environment are endless. As a result, every day I push myself to squeeze all the juice out of every opportunity, and over the years I have been rewarded for my high level of engagement.

On October 6, 2014, I found myself at the San Francisco airport on my way to Norway. This trip came on the heels of a whirlwind trip to New York City, where I'd barely slept because the hotel was so noisy. My new destination was the Arctic Circle, where I was to run a workshop for a group of young entrepreneurs. As I waited for the flight, I had the sudden conviction that I shouldn't get on the plane. I was completely exhausted and feared that this trip would take me to my knees. A colleague with whom I was traveling, and to whom I expressed my reservations, looked at me with surprise. Was I really going to bail on this trip? Of course not. I got on the plane.

When I got to Norway, after three long flights, my colleague and I delivered the workshop and made the long journey home. Due to jet lag, I hadn't slept in days and was totally drained. I got back to California on a Sunday night and was scheduled to run a three-hour workshop for a group from Brazil on Monday morning. I met the group as planned, but my mind was swimming and my body ached as I ran the session.

Essentially, my plate was so full that I felt like I was choking. I was scared by this, but I didn't know how to slow down. Each day I continued to deliver on my long list of commitments—and took on more—while I felt more and more fatigued and disoriented. Fighting off daily panic attacks, I desperately tried to keep my heart rate under control.

On October 30, I was to run a workshop on creative problem solving that I had volunteered to lead at San Quentin prison. My husband, Mike, went with me. Before the session started, I turned to Mike and said, "I'm really sick." He asked if we should leave, but I said no. I wanted to run the workshop, and I gave it all I had.

On the way home I started having severe heart palpitations, and I couldn't breathe. I asked Mike to take me to the hospital. We raced down the highway to the Stanford Hospital emergency room, where doctors did endless tests, including an X-ray, an ultrasound, a CT scan, and blood tests. There was nothing wrong with me, they concluded, except that my heart was racing out of control and my blood pressure was through the roof. At two in the morning they released me. The next day, I stayed home in the morning but insisted on going to work for a long-planned meeting with my colleagues in the afternoon.

The following day was Saturday. That morning I walked upstairs with Mike to measure the windows in our bathroom for some new shutters. My heart started racing faster and faster, until I collapsed on the floor. I couldn't breathe, and I felt sick to my stomach. Mike threw on his shoes and rushed me back to the ER, where they kept me under observation all day. The verdict: my symptoms were the result of total exhaustion, stress, and anxiety.

On Monday, my primary care physician took one look at me and ordered me on a one-month medical leave. During my recovery, I had lots of time for thoughtful reflection on the trade-offs between persistence and survival, and I came up with a metaphor that captures what I learned from this experience. It is as follows:

Each of us is sailing a sturdy sailboat across an ocean. We're free to navigate as we wish, influenced by the winds of the world. There are some days with calm water and others with big waves; and there are days with bright sunshine and others with stormy weather. The boat is designed to withstand all of these. Rain and rivers replenish evaporating ocean water, keeping the system in balance.

At the bottom of the ocean are mountains. You can't see them unless the water level drops too low, and they don't influence the currents when the ocean is full. Trouble occurs, though, when the ocean gets depleted due to lack of rain or water from rivers. You can fool yourself into thinking things are fine as the water gets lower and lower. However, eventually your sailboat hits bottom and gets stuck on the rocks.

The water is your reserves, and the mountains are your weakest links. You build up your reserves by taking care of yourself—getting enough rest, eating well, exercising, and spending time with friends and family. The mountains represent the first things that happen when you get stressed, including anxiety, stomachaches, sleeplessness, headaches, or a sore throat.

When you hit bottom, you can do two things to recover: build up your reserves and/or learn how to sail around the mountains. You refill the ocean by slowly getting recharged, and bypass the mountains by learning how to cope with stress. Both of these take time and effort, as does repairing your damaged sailboat. It is obviously much better to avoid hitting bottom. This requires a dedication to taking care of yourself, paying attention to the "water level," and preparing for inevitable droughts.

It takes persistence to bring your ideas to life. You need to set goals, focus on a task for an extended period of time, and push through obstacles along the way, all of which require both mental and physical grit. However, this is not enough. You need to replenish your reserves along the way by taking care of yourself so that you have the physical and mental energy to achieve your goals. Each day is a step toward your future, and the choices you make today determine the opportunities you have tomorrow.

## Projects

---

1. Make a list of all the resources you have. Start with the obvious things and then dig down to identify other tangible and intangible resources available to you.

2. Take a few "steps" this week that are a bit larger than you think you can handle. For example, volunteer to do something that will take more effort than you usually expend, or tackle a problem that looks complicated at first glance. Afterward, spend some time on reflection. Were the results as you expected, or were you able to handle the larger step gracefully?

3. How high is your "ocean"? How far below the surface are the mountains? Can you identify the specific mountains that are closest to the surface? What are you doing to stay replenished? What more *could* you do?

# Chapter 8

# Inspire

## *Tell Me a Story*

Most significant accomplishments are like barn raisings—you can't do them yourself. They require a collection of individuals who are dedicated to the success of the project. Therefore, if you want to accomplish something of merit, you need to find ways to magnify your impact by influencing others to support your efforts. This involves encouraging others to join your team, fund your work, use your products, and spread the word. This is equally true for artists, musicians, chefs, technology innovators, and other entrepreneurs who want to reach a broader audience.

There are several helpful models that describe how people inspire others to join their cause, amplifying their reach.

Each provides a different perspective on recruiting others to help you reach your objectives.

The first, developed by Liz Wiseman and Greg McKeown, focuses on "multipliers"—people who enhance the creativity and productivity of their organization. Multipliers are those who attract terrific talent by creating an environment that motivates others to do their best work. They do this by providing bold challenges that stretch others' imagination, creating a culture of constructive debate, and giving ownership and credit to those who contribute. This collection of behaviors leads to vastly increased morale and motivation and generates a quantum leap in output. Wiseman and McKeown write, "Simply put, when you invite people's best thinking and lead like a multiplier, your team will give you more—more discretionary effort, more mental and physical energy, and more of the fresh ideas critical for long-term success."

At the other extreme are "diminishers"—people who inhibit creativity and productivity by building their own personal empire, hoarding resources, giving directives that don't leave room for others to contribute, micromanaging, and making all the decisions. When you suppress others' freedom of expression, you get a fraction of their effort and output.

The starting point for multipliers is enticing talented people to join your team. One of the most powerful tools for doing so is telling a compelling story that captures your vision. Inspiring stories motivate others to join your cause, even when it wasn't their original idea. Most people are hungry to be inspired by other people's stories and are eager to join in. This is the crucial link between entrepreneurship and imagination in the Invention Cycle. Organizations of all types, from preschools to research laboratories, are filled with people who are passionate about what they're doing, motivated by the vision of colleagues who have inspired their imagination.

Companies, as well as individuals, have stories. If a company's story is compelling, it generates a wide swath of support and interest. If not, the prospects are diminished. Venture capitalist Ben Horowitz says, "Companies that don't have a clearly articulated story don't have a clear and well thought-out strategy. . . . The company story *is* the company strategy." Your company story needs to clearly tell what you are doing and why. Communicating this in an engaging way is fundamental to effective leadership. "The story must explain at a fundamental level why you exist. Why does the world need your company? Why do we need to be doing what we're doing and why is it important?" This harks back to the discussion in chapter 3 on motivation, because your story directly reflects your motivation.

According to Chip and Dan Heath, coauthors of *Made to Stick,* there are several core principles for stories that are really compelling (and thus "sticky"). The stories must be easy to understand, have a surprising element, and be both believable and emotionally charged. We're drawn in by these stories and want to pass them on to others. Whether you're making a toothbrush or a drinking water filter, the more engaging your story, the more likely people will be to join you.

In the summer of 2014, the Ice Bucket Challenge to support research for a cure for ALS (also known as Lou Gehrig's disease) went viral. The story was simple and very sticky: Individuals filmed themselves dumping a bucket of ice water over their heads, and posted that video online. They then nominated three other people to do the same. Those who didn't do it, needed to make a charitable donation to the ALS Association. This challenge raised awareness about ALS among the millions of people who participated, and millions more who saw the videos. It also raised over $40 million in a couple of months, far more than the organization had raised in prior years.

The key to the "virality" of the Ice Bucket Challenge was its simplicity (what could be simpler than pouring a bucket of ice water on your head?), the surprise factor (an ice bath isn't something you would usually choose), and the fact that people are compelled to pass it along to others (once you complete the challenge yourself, you pass it on to three specific people). Most people who partook didn't even know about ALS before they received the challenge, but they learned about this debilitating illness because the challenge was fast, provocative, and easy to spread in a short video posted on social media sites. The multiplier effect was huge! According to the *New York Times,* between June 1 and August 13 there were more than 1.2 million Ice Bucket Challenge videos viewed on Facebook, and more than 2.2 million mentions on Twitter. In addition, donations to the ALS Association hit

$41.8 million, more than double the amount the association had received during the prior year.

We consume stories all day long, when we read them in the newspaper, when we watch shows and commercials on TV, and when we listen to programming on the radio. In addition, each of us tells a story every time we share what we're doing with a friend, family member, colleague, investor, lawyer, or doctor. When you tell your doctor about your symptoms, they're embedded in a story about your life. When you talk to your lawyer about a situation where you've been wronged, you are telling a story about the infringement. The stories we tell reveal much about us, and it is incumbent upon each of us to learn how to tell stories that have the impact we hope to achieve. Since we tell stories so frequently, we have lots of opportunities to practice.

A case in point: When I interview job candidates, I always begin by asking them to tell me their story. The results are invariably illuminating. Their response quickly unlocks their view of the world and reveals how they see themselves. Some stories focus on how fortunate candidates have been, some focus on their bad luck, some concentrate on how hard they've worked to get where they are, and some reveal a random walk through life. By hearing the stories, I can easily visualize how well or poorly each candidate will look at the new role and at the possibilities that it holds.

In chapter 7, on persistence, I shared a particularly difficult time in my life when I struggled with exhaustion and anxiety. During this time my mind was drawn to dark thoughts that were terribly distressing. When I finally admitted that I couldn't go on as I had been, I made the active decision to change my story. So I sat down and literally wrote a new one. I crafted a few pages that described my life two years in the future and explained what I had done to get me from here to there. The new story provided a road map and helped me navigate the path forward.

We each have a story of our life that we carry with us, and it influences how we engage with each new experience. If I asked you to tell your complete life story in as much detail as possible, it would probably take an hour or so. If you wrote a book conveying your life story, it might take a dozen hours to read—less than one day of your life. We continually distill our story down to a collection of pivotal moments that we believe represent who we are. We choose which episodes to include and how we frame them. Those stories say a great deal about us, but they also shape the way in which we engage with the world, and as a result how the world engages with us.

I remember running into an old friend who had worked with me many years earlier. We started trading stories of our shared experiences. It was fascinating how differently we remembered our time together. He recalled a long list of incidents in which he and others had been treated badly. I didn't remember any of that. My memories were much less bittersweet; I found humor in some of the scenarios that he still found terribly frustrating. If you didn't know that we'd worked in the same company, you'd never have guessed it from our recollections. The two of us clearly have very different ways of looking at the world, as evidenced by the completely different stories we told of that earlier time.

The same is true in families. Each child experiences things differently, the siblings essentially living parallel childhoods in the same house. Our varying perspectives determine which stories we tell. By deliberately shifting our frame of reference, we can see completely different things in real time and in retrospect. This draws upon the skills discussed in chapter 6, on reframing.

Neuroscientist, David Eagleman has written a book called *Sum,* in which each chapter describes a fanciful version of what happens after we die. In the particularly provocative final chapter, he describes a scenario in which we finally see our entire life clearly—or so we think—when we get to the end of our lives. Then, after we die, we see our life again in reverse. This time we realize that everything we believed was in fact incorrect. When we see our journey from a different perspective, from the end to the beginning, each episode looks completely different. This is similar to the Christopher Nolan film *Memento* in which one of the characters has no long-term memory. The story plays out backward to create a similar feeling in the audience. As earlier scenes are revealed, the audience realizes that their interpretations of what happened before are all wrong. Both of these tales remind us that we're always interpreting everything, and continually composing a story that holds our interpretations together.

An effective story always leaves room for the person who is consuming it. There has to be enough detail to make the narrative compelling, but not so much that it squeezes out the audience. Effective fiction stories, music, and art leave room for readers, listeners, and viewers to fill in the gaps with their imagination. When companies recruit new employees, the stories recruiters tell need to leave room for job candidates to make important contributions. In a discussion I had with John Hennessy, president of Stanford University, he said that the most effective initiatives at the university are not born fully formed, but leave room for others to add their ideas. The basic vision is set, but the initiative can be molded by those who join the team. This resonates with Wiseman and McKeown's concept of multipliers—they leave space for others to contribute.

In my classes, students are required to share their work using various storytelling techniques. They learn how to use a variety of frameworks that provide a structure for a story, which makes their presentations much more meaningful to the audience. No matter how innovative their ideas, if those ideas aren't presented in a compelling way, nobody will care. That's why advertisers use stories to sell products. We are drawn in by the narrative, which attracts us to the product.

A great example comes from Skype, which developed the strategy of telling user stories to build awareness and passion for the product. David Aaker, marketing expert, describes the goal and the impact of those stories. Here is one example:

> Erin Van Oordt, a nurse on a mission in a poverty-stricken village in rural Guatemala, came across Jenri Rivera, a deaf 7-year-old boy with a bright smile. Against all odds she enlisted an ear surgeon, the director of Ray of Hope Medical Mission, a device maker Advanced Bionics, and others to give Jenri, who had never even had a medical checkup, a chance at hearing. After the operation, Jenri waved to his Skype-connected parents on the other end of a laptop screen and for the first time heard them speak. Erin burst into tears of happiness.

This story was shared as part of a new Skype program, called "Build User Love." The company uses formal training sessions and newsletters to teach employees to recognize effective stories and how to create them to spread the word about the impact of their product.

Even when giving a formal talk, such as a Ph.D. defense or a business pitch, it is powerful to use a story to engage your audience and inspire them to take action, whether it's signing off on your graduate thesis or offering a term sheet. All successful stories begin with a compelling hook that engages the emotions of the audience. The hook can be a provocative question, a quote, or a joke that sets the stage for the rest of the story. Each story also needs a structure, just as a house does. Famous author Kurt Vonnegut describes several different story shapes and provides examples of books and movies that use each structure. We are very tuned to these structures, which engage our emotions along the way. Below is an infographic, designed by Maya Eilam, showing a few of the story shapes described by Vonnegut.

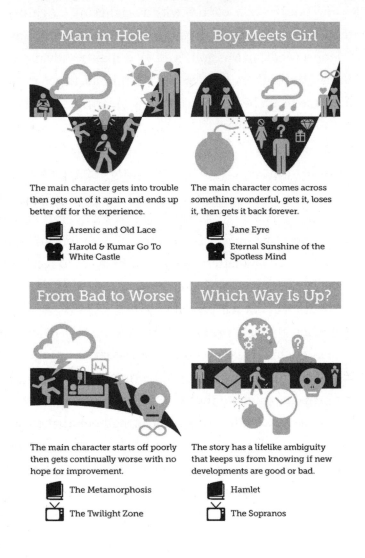

- **Man in Hole**

  The main character gets into trouble then gets out of it again and ends up better off for the experience.

  - Arsenic and Old Lace
  - Harold & Kumar Go To White Castle

- **Boy Meets Girl**

  The main character comes across something wonderful, gets it, loses it, then gets it back forever.

  - Jane Eyre
  - Eternal Sunshine of the Spotless Mind

- **From Bad to Worse**

  The main character starts off poorly then gets continually worse with no hope for improvement.

  - The Metamorphosis
  - The Twilight Zone

- **Which Way Is Up?**

  The story has a lifelike ambiguity that keeps us from knowing if new developments are good or bad.

  - Hamlet
  - The Sopranos

The simple "story spine" structure, first described by playwright and performer, Ken Adams, is an easy and very useful framework. It is as follows:

*Once upon a time* . . . (introduce situation)
*Every day* . . . (add details)
*But one day* . . . (something that breaks the routine)
*Because of that* . . . (consequence 1)
*Because of that* . . . (consequence 2)
*Because of that* . . . (consequence 3), etc.
*Until finally* . . . (the climax)
*And ever since then* . . . (resolution)

This framework is the backbone of most fairy tales. Ken Adams shows how it can be applied to *The Wizard of Oz*:

*Once upon a time,* there was a little girl named Dorothy who was carried by a tornado to the magical land of Oz.
*Every day,* she journeyed toward the Emerald City in order to ask the Great and Powerful Wizard of Oz to help her get home.
*But one day,* she got to Oz and she met the Wizard.
*Because of that,* the Wizard told Dorothy that he would only help her get home if she killed the Wicked Witch of the West.
*Because of that,* Dorothy encountered many dangers and was finally successful in destroying the witch.
*Because of that,* the Wizard agreed to take Dorothy home in his hot-air balloon.

*Until finally,* on the day of their departure, Dorothy ran
  after her dog, Toto, and missed the balloon.
*And ever since then,* Dorothy learned that she always had
  the power to get home on her own, which she did.

He notes that, "when stripped down to the story spine, the movie in question loses many of its characters and much of what makes it so brilliant and memorable. That's because the story spine is *not* the story, it's the spine. It's nothing but the bare-boned structure upon which the story is built. And, that's what makes it such a powerful tool. It allows you, as a writer, to look at your story at its structural core and to ensure that the basic building blocks are all in the right place."

This structure can also be used in an effective business pitch. Here's an example of how it might work as scaffolding for a product pitch for Cala Health, a startup described in detail in the introduction to this book:

*Once upon a time,* eight million Americans suffered from
  hand tremors.
*Every day,* they had trouble with simple tasks, such as
  drinking a cup of coffee and buttoning their shirt.
*But one day,* Cala Health developed an inexpensive,
  noninvasive treatment that eliminated their hand
  tremors.
*Because of that,* there was an effective and affordable
  alternative to invasive brain surgery.

*Because of that,* many more people were able to get
   treatment for their condition.
*Because of that,* they became able to take care of
   themselves more easily.
*Until finally,* this new treatment became the standard of
   care for treating hand tremors.
*And ever since then,* millions of people have been able to
   live without debilitating symptoms.

One of easiest ways to check the effectiveness of your story
is by using the "bar test" described by Nicole Kahn, a senior
project lead at the design firm IDEO. Essentially, she and her
colleagues practice telling the story of a new product or service as though they were telling someone at a bar, without
any fancy slides or data.

Running the bar test involves talking to people, often
strangers, and getting their quick feedback on an idea. According to Nicole,

> We tell them our story. We verbalize it. We grab a col-
> league who's completely unfamiliar with what we're
> doing and buy them a beer or a coffee and spend 15 min-
> utes to see if they understand the point of the presenta-
> tion. . . . We look for when they lean in, or when they look
> away or reach for their phone. We look for nods and "uh
> huhs"—we look for what surprises and delights. That's
> how we figure out what's sticky and resonating. . . . Force
> it to be succinct. That's the magic of verbalizing your

story. You've invested nothing and there's no reason to get stuck. You can redo it again and again.

Key goals for your story should be first to resonate with the passions of your audience and then to give them a clear path for action. Bob Sutton and Huggy Rao discuss this in their book, *Scaling Up Excellence*. They describe the need for a "hot" cause and a "cool" solution. When you trigger an emotional response in people, they stop thinking about themselves and start thinking about the collective interest. Bob and Huggy describe the 2006 initiative by the Institute for Healthcare Improvement, called the 100,000 Lives Campaign, with the mission of encouraging doctors and nurses to adopt practices that lead to much better patient outcomes. The actions include six very simple steps, such as washing hands between visiting patients. To launch the campaign, the leaders of the initiative held a conference with four thousand members of the medical community. One of the speakers was Sorrel King, who had lost her daughter to a preventable medical error. Her impassioned plea to never let this happen again ignited the audience's enthusiasm and mobilized them to adopt the six simple practices. This, in turn, saved over one hundred thousand lives. This is an example of a hot cause (saving lives), followed by a cool solution (washing hands).

In his book *Influence: The Psychology of Persuasion*, Robert Cialdini outlines six approaches for infecting others with your ideas: reciprocity, consistency, social proof, liking, authority, and scarcity. Let's look at an example to see how an effective leader employs these tools to influence others and to engage them in an important cause. I've selected an example close to home, where I have access to seeing this influence at work.

The Stanford Technology Ventures Program took on a big challenge in 2011. Supported by the National Science Foundation, STVP was charged with infusing innovation and entrepreneurial thinking into engineering education across the United States. The new initiative was to be called Epicenter: National Center for Engineering Pathways to Innovation. With an ambitious goal, a collection of academic directors who had not worked together before, and a team that was spread across the country, the project got off to a rocky start. There were so many points of view and personality differences that it was nearly impossible to get everyone on the same page. In fact, the project was at serious risk of failing during the first year. With so much to gain if successful, and so much to lose if not, the team had a pressing need to become aligned, engaged, mobilized, and headed in the same direction. Essentially, the Epicenter needed an entrepreneurial leader to inspire others to share and execute a consistent vision and plan.

Tom Byers, Epicenter director, stepped up to the task. Working with the project's non-profit partner, VentureWell, and its CEO Phil Weilerstein, Tom consciously drew upon Cialdini's framework for guidance on how to harness the diverse talents of those on the entire team.

He started with *consistency,* asking everyone to publicly commit to delivering specific contributions to the project. Public commitments result in much higher follow-through rates. Tom made sure that everyone agreed to a clear set of goals and deliverables.

Tom then used *reciprocity,* reaching out to help others on the team become successful. He listened to each person's requests and concerns, and found ways to get each person what he or she needed. In turn, team members felt obliged to help Tom when he reached out for a favor.

Tom modeled the behavior that he wanted others to mirror. This provided *social proof* that the behavior was both acceptable and expected. He demonstrated the type of communications he wanted from the team, and modeled giving frequent positive feedback for projects that were completed well and on time.

The fourth Cialdini principle Tom used is *liking.* People are much more willing to follow those that they admire and trust. Tom built a personal relationship with each person on the team, learning each of his or her motivations and special needs.

As the principal investigator on the project, Tom knew that he had the mandate to tell people what to do. He used this tool, *authority,* as a last resort, but everyone knew that he had this power if he wanted to use it.

Tom used *scarcity* by making it clear that there were limited funds for each of the Epicenter initiatives. We are drawn to things that are in short supply, such as the last ticket to a concert or a special offer that will soon expire. Each team had to convince the others that their project was deserving of funds. By arguing on their own behalf for the resources, they bolstered their commitment to their respective projects.

Inspiring others to act is not about getting people to do the things *you* want them to do, but motivating *them* to want to do those things. To that end, we can supplement Cialdini's six tools with presence, warmth, and power—described by Olivia Fox Cabane in her book *The Charisma Myth*.

*Presence,* Olivia says, is the core of charisma. We all recognize when we're with someone who is distracted and clearly *not* present. This lack of focus instantly destroys his or her charisma. Think of how you feel when someone looks at his or her cell phone in the middle of a conversation, or glances over your shoulder to see if there is someone more important in the room. Those with presence never do such things. They behave as though *you* are the only person in the room, and everyone and everything else has evaporated. No one can fake presence, because it's obvious if a person isn't fully engaged.

The second component of charisma, in Olivia's view, is *warmth*. This is essentially the impression that someone likes you and will use his or her power on your behalf. We sense warmth primarily via body language and eye contact.

Those who don't look us in the eye, for example, we perceive as being colder than those who hold our gaze.

Finally, charisma involves *power,* as described by Olivia:

Power is your perception of your ability to affect the world around you. Whether this be through raw physical power, or large amounts of money, influence, expertise, intelligence, high social status and so forth. We look for clues of power in the person's appearance, in others' reaction to that person, but most of all in the person's demeanor in their body language. . . . The MIT Media Lab was able to predict the outcome of negotiations, sales calls, and business plan pitches with 87% accuracy without listening to a single word of content, only by analyzing the voice fluctuation and the facial expression of the person pitching.

You control your own charisma and can practice the skills related to power, presence, and warmth. Once you start paying attention, you will see how people display or dissipate their charisma by the way they stand or sit, the manner in which they talk, the expression on their face, and their use or lack of full engagement.

Aleta Hayes, who teaches dance at Stanford, says that we are "always already dancing." That is, we are always moving in the world, and others interpret that as our "dance." I have been fortunate to teach with Aleta in many situations and have observed her transform people before my eyes by helping them unlock their presence, warmth, and power. She illustrated this transformation beautifully while running a workshop on physical presence. Aleta demonstrated two ways to enter a room. In the first, she walked in casually and looked around. In the second, she walked in deliberately, planted her feet firmly and gracefully, stood up straight, and made warm eye contact with others in the room. The difference was so dramatic that it moved me to tears. She literally transformed herself from nobody to somebody in seconds.

This chapter has described several ways to encourage others to help scale your efforts. These include creating an environment that multiplies the output of your team, telling a "sticky" story that compels others to join you, framing your story so that it has the greatest impact, using storytelling techniques—such as the story spine—to communicate your ideas, using principles of influence to compel others to action, and bolstering your charisma to increase your effectiveness. Whether you know it consciously or not, you're influencing others in every one of your interactions.

Inspiring collaborators, customers, investors, family members, and friends is a key role of an entrepreneur, no matter what your pursuit. It is nearly impossible to manifest your ideas, whether you're an artist or an astronaut, if other people don't share your dream and support your effort. This doesn't mean that *everyone* needs to embrace your ideas. But you do need a critical mass of avid supporters to amplify the impact of your vision. This is why inspiration is the keystone of the Invention Cycle. It provides the spark that leads to the next wave upon wave of imagination, creativity, innovation, and entrepreneurship.

## Projects

1. Tell or write your life story three times. The first time, focus on all the terrible things that have happened to you. The next time, focus on all the wonderful opportunities you've had. And the third time, tell your story as a comedian would, finding the humor in every episode.

2. Use the story spine framework to tell several stories. Practice presenting these stories to your friends, family, and/or colleagues.

3. Consider your own presence, warmth, and power. Which of these characteristics do you exhibit, and which could be enhanced? Pay attention to those around you and privately evaluate their presence, warmth, and power. How do these traits affect you and others?

# Conclusion

## *The End Is the Beginning*

After dozens of interviews with successful entrepreneurs across a wide range of disciplines, I've seen the Invention Cycle play out again and again. The stages take differing amounts of time, depending upon the problem that is being addressed, but the pattern is consistent. Among others, I shared the Invention Cycle model with Sal Khan, founder of the online Khan Academy, and he agreed that this was the path he had followed as he built his venture:

In 2004, Sal worked in Boston as a financial analyst for a hedge fund. His young cousin in New Orleans was struggling in math so he started tutoring her remotely over the phone. A year into this, Sal began making math practice software for her, which he shared with all his other cousins who were also eager to take advantage of his free tutoring. A year later, he started making short videos, which he posted on YouTube, to complement the math software. His cousins found them incredibly useful, as did many others who just happened to find them. Inspired by the impact he was having, Sal considered how he might scale the process of making educational videos to address a wider audience. This was the *imagination* stage, where Sal became *engaged* with teaching and *envisioned* something new.

By the time Sal had posted thirty to forty videos, letters were pouring in. Kids wrote, thanking him for helping them master subjects they'd thought they would never learn, and parents sent their thanks for helping their children succeed in school. Sal's drive to build educational content blossomed, and he tried various teaching and technical approaches to see which worked best. This was the *creativity* stage, which required both *motivation* and *experimentation*.

By 2009, three years after he started posting videos, about one hundred thousand people were using Sal's content each month! With this success, he left his job in finance to commit his full-time effort to online education. Sal knew enough to question conventional teaching methods, and he built a unique learning platform that he called Khan Academy. This was the *innovation* stage, which required both *focusing* and *reframing* to come up with fresh ideas.

As his vision grew, Sal needed to bring in financial support, hire employees, and encourage more people to use the Khan Academy resources. Sal's tenacity and ability to mobilize others helped him galvanize a great team, develop partnerships, and compel donors to support his effort. He entered the *entrepreneurship* stage, which required both *persistence* and the ability to *inspire* others. His work has had a far-reaching impact around the world, sparking the imagination of students, educators, and other entrepreneurs.

As this example illustrates, by building the scaffolding that supports bringing your *own* ideas to life, you in turn create a platform for *others* to do the same. This is the essence of the Invention Cycle.

Individual Invention Cycle          Collective Invention Cycle

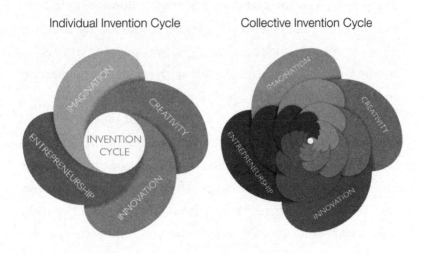

As described in the previous chapters, there is an effective pathway through this process, from inspiration to implementation, with a requisite set of attitudes and actions:

- Imagination requires active *engagement* and the ability to *envision* alternatives.

- Creativity requires *motivation* and *experimentation* to address challenges.

- Innovation requires *focusing* and *reframing* to generate unique solutions.

- Entrepreneurship requires *persistence* and the ability to *inspire* others.

It is important to keep in mind that your attitudes are impotent unless you develop behaviors that bring those thoughts to fruition; and your actions are doomed to fail unless they are paired with the proper mind-set. By braiding together your attitudes and actions, you prepare yourself to do much more than is imaginable with much less than seems possible, no matter your objective.

Looking at the Invention Cycle from that perspective, you can see that those who manifest the required attitudes are *effective,* and those who have the requisite actions are *inventive.* Effectiveness is your ability to get things done, and inventiveness allows you to generate breakout ideas. Each set of traits is necessary but not sufficient—only when they are coupled together are you effective at bringing new ideas to fruition.

| *Attitudes for Effectiveness* | *Actions for Inventiveness* |
| --- | --- |
| Engaged | Envisioning |
| Motivated | Experimenting |
| Focused | Reframing |
| Persistent | Inspiring |

The Invention Cycle supports and reinforces other models related to innovation and entrepreneurship, including the design thinking process, developed by my colleagues at Stanford's d.school, and taught widely around the world.

Design thinking usually refers to five steps for generating ideas:

---

*Observe* → *Define* → *Ideate* →
*Prototype* → *Test*

---

Tim Brown, the president and CEO of the design firm IDEO, defines design thinking as "a human-centered approach to innovation that draws from the designer's toolkit to integrate the needs of people, the possibilities of technology, and the requirements for business success." Using this process, design thinkers make careful observations from a specific point of view and, based upon their insights, frame a specific problem that needs to be addressed. For example, they might observe a hospital stay from the perspective of a patient and then frame a problem such as, "How might we create a way for patients to get a good night's sleep in a room with lots of noisy machines that monitor their condition?"

Design thinkers then ideate to generate a large set of possible solutions. Many of those solutions are tested using low-resolution prototypes—or pretypes—that are presented to potential users to get feedback. For example, designers might mock up special headphones for patients that block out the noise, or create a prototype of a machine that plays music in rhythms that match the heartbeat, as opposed to beeping loudly.

Design thinking provides a collection of skills that are most effective when used in concert. For example, it's important to ideate while defining the problem you will tackle. And it's productive to continue observing to get more insights throughout the design process. The linear process is useful to a person learning the requisite skills, but experienced design thinkers use this model as a guide, not a recipe. The same is true for the Invention Cycle. Once you master the skills at each stage, you continue to use them in combination throughout your entrepreneurial journey. They form a scaffolding of attitudes and actions that support the *entire* entrepreneurial process.

The Invention Cycle builds on the design thinking framework in three ways:

1. The Invention Cycle differentiates between creativity and innovation: the former leads to expected solutions, and the latter results in breakthrough ideas. This is an important distinction that encourages you to push beyond incremental ideas while generating ideas at each stage of the design thinking process.

2. The Invention Cycle takes attitude into account. Your mind-set has a strong influence on the creative process and must be considered. The more engaged, motivated, focused, and persistent you are, the more likely you will be to generate real innovation and to overcome obstacles along the path toward implementation.

3. The Invention Cycle also includes the implementation stage, in which ideas are manifest in the world, which requires persistence and inspiring others. This is an important step in that it not only allows ideas to scale, but also inspires others' imagination to start the cycle anew.

The Invention Cycle also provides foundational skills for the "lean startup" process, described by both Steve Blank and Eric Ries. Their models encourage startups to use rapid experimentation with feedback from customers to hone product development. Both have shown that proponents of any venture can reduce the risk of failure and the need for large amounts of initial funding by iteratively building products and services that meet the needs of their customers.

Steve Blank, who has built a highly successful program that teaches the lean startup methodology to thousands of teams around the world, realizes that many people come to his workshops with the goal of starting a venture but have no idea where to begin. His model starts *after* defining the problem you want to solve, and have an initial idea for a solution. Here is his take on how the Invention Cycle supports the lean startup process:

> The Lean Startup is a process for turning ideas into commercial ventures. Its premise is that startups begin with a series of untested hypotheses. They succeed by getting out of the building, testing those hypotheses and learning by iterating and refining minimal viable products in front of potential customers.
>
> That's all well and good if you already have an idea. But where do startup ideas come from? Where do inspiration, imagination and creativity come to bear? How does that all relate to innovation and entrepreneurship?
>
> It troubled me that the practice of entrepreneurship was missing a set of tools to unleash my students' imaginations and lacked a process to apply their creativity. I realized the innovation/entrepreneurship process needed a "foundation"—the skills and processes that kick-start an entrepreneur's imagination and creative juices. We needed to define the language and pieces that make up an "entrepreneurial mind-set."

In essence, the Invention Cycle provides both the starting point for all entrepreneurial ventures and guideposts along the way. It gives you tools for generating bold ideas as well as a road map for navigating the pathway from inspiration to implementation. As a result, the Invention Cycle allows you to identify more opportunities, generate unique solutions, and manifest your ideas—important skills for designing and implementing the life you want to lead.

If you've completed the projects outlined at the end of each chapter, you will by now have identified some meaningful opportunities and crafted a bold goal for yourself. You will have a clearer picture of what motivates you and understand the relationship between your confidence and your passions. You will also have identified potential hurdles along the way, including those inside and outside yourself. In addition, you will have mastered a collection of tools for testing your ideas, increasing your focus and persistence, looking at old things in new ways, and inspiring others to support and join your cause. Finally, you will have gained an understanding of the importance of taking care of yourself, making sure that you stay replenished throughout your journey.

These skills and attitudes should be taught to *everyone*. What could be more important than preparing people to envision and then live the life they want to lead? There are a growing number of opportunities to learn these skills. As described in chapter 3, Don Wettrick is sharing them with his high school students. In addition, many schools around the world are now incorporating classes on design thinking and problem-based learning. Founder of Tribewanted, Ben Keene compiled a list of interesting examples in an article called "Schools for Life." His list includes Right to Dream in

Ghana, Kaos Pilots in Denmark, DO School in Berlin, Green School in Bali, THNK in Amsterdam and Vancouver, and School of Life in London.

I am fortunate to be involved with a relatively new program, Draper University, targeting young people age eighteen to twenty-eight. Founded in 2013 and led by Tim Draper, a venture capitalist whose firms, Draper Fisher Jurvetson and Draper Associates, have invested in firms such as Tesla, Skype, Theranos, Baidu and SpaceX, the program is designed to prepare participants to be heroes in their own lives. Set in a historic hotel in downtown San Mateo, California, Draper University is anything but a traditional school. It is an experiential, eight-week program to which participants are drawn because they are eager to tap into their entrepreneurial spirit. Some come to learn how to launch new ventures, and others to learn how to launch their own lives.

The first floor of the building has open, flexible space surrounded by white-board walls and filled with colorful beanbag chairs. They call this the "egg room." On each of the upper floors is a painting of a superhero, from Wonder Woman to Superman. These images are there to inspire the young participants to see themselves as heroes who can accomplish remarkable feats.

During the program, participants read science fiction novels to learn how to envision a brand-new future, and they take on physical and mental challenges that take them way outside their comfort zone. They learn business skills such as branding and selling, as well as negotiation and lie-detection.

They also learn about cutting-edge technology and ideas, such as 3-D printing and virtual reality. Each day, they meet with people who have made their mark in a wide range of fields, and they learn that these people are no different than they are. During a survival weekend, they learn everything from first aid and suturing, to how to live off the land. In parallel, they are working on their own business ideas and learn how to pitch them to a panel of experts at the end of the program. At the core, Draper University teaches students that a key to their success is having a bold goal and the tenacity to reach it.

You can also teach yourself these skills. There are countless role models of those who have taken on an audacious goal and built a path to that objective. Many of the cases in this book tell the story of people who did just that. Like Sal Khan, who developed Khan Academy, and Piya Sorcar, who is addressing AIDS education in India and beyond, you can build your skills organically by following the process described in the Invention Cycle, beginning with engagement and envisioning what might be. With motivation to propel you forward, the experimentation begins, leading to opportunities to see challenges with fresh eyes. Once you identify your unique contribution, it takes persistence to manifest those ideas and to inspire others to join you on your journey.

It is clear that people around the world are hungry to tap into their vast potential and are eager to carve a path to a compelling future. Since *What I Wish I Knew When I Was 20* and *inGenius* were released in 2009 and 2012, respectively, I've received well over a thousand letters from people all over the world with these messages. Whether they're in Japan, Korea, Thailand, Russia, Israel, Turkey, Brazil, or Africa, they yearn to do something meaningful with their life and are urgently looking for tools to help them do so. Some have faced palpable external pressures, such as limited resources and messaging about what they are expected to achieve; and others deal with internal struggles, such as a lack of confidence that they can reach their goals. The Invention Cycle is designed to build on my prior work, providing a road map for integrating your attitudes and actions in order to manifest the life you hope to lead.

I began this book with a letter that I wrote to myself on the eve of my twentieth birthday, and I'll finish with a note from one of my students. In this, his final reflection at the completion of our course, he uses the story spine format to share what he took from our class experience:

> *Once upon a time* there was a student named Hussain. He was an average kid, and most who met him spent most of their initial conversation wondering how he could have been admitted to Stanford.
> *And, every quarter,* in order to mask his inadequacies, Hussain would sign up for very difficult courses

with extremely technical descriptions, regardless of his interests.

*Until one quarter,* his senior year, Hussain decided he would select classes based upon how interesting he found them, not how hard they sounded to his friends.

*Because of that,* he ended up in some super random classes, including Engineering Innovation.

*Because of that,* he was so engaged in class that Hussain started applying the principles he was learning to other aspects of his life.

*Because of that,* he got more and more experience practicing skills, such as how to reframe problems and challenge assumptions, and how to tell a compelling story.

*Because of that,* Hussain began to view life less as a casual participant and more as an active innovator.

*Until finally,* he became much more present in each moment.

*Ever since then,* the lessons remain. The most important one is that inspiration and happiness are most easily found doing what you really want to do, and not what you think you should do. Your future is determined by how you dance in the present.

Hussain's story reinforces the message that your attitudes and actions are inextricably intertwined. They fuel each other, igniting a powerful chain reaction that leads to wave upon wave of ideas and actions. If you actively shape your mind-set and hone your behavior, there is no end to this cycle and no limit to what you can achieve. You are the master of your Invention Cycle, where the end is just the beginning.

## Projects

1. Return to the letter you wrote about your goals for yourself. Edit the letter again. This time include all the attitudes and actions that are required at each stage of the Invention Cycle.

2. Having gone through this process, make a list of your key insights. What did you already know and what is new? How will what you've learned influence your attitudes and actions going forward?

# Summary of Projects

## Setting Goals

Write a letter to yourself describing what you hope to achieve in the future. Select the timeframe that makes the most sense to you, and be as specific as you like. The goal of this exercise is to get you into the mind-set of thinking about carving a path toward your objectives. There will be opportunities to revisit the letter in chapter 2 and again at the end, so please consider it a draft that will be revised.

## Identifying Opportunities

Spend an hour silently observing in one location. It can be anywhere—a café, your office, a city street, a park, or at home. Make as many observations as possible. Consider the implications of these observations, and identify as many opportunities as you can.

Look up job listings in your area, even if you have a job. Select three completely different jobs and write a paragraph that describes the possible paths forward, starting with the advertised role.

# Envisioning the Future

Make up your own story, using the illustration by Kevin Meier on page 41.

Think of the world as a collection of stages, from your hometown to the entire world. Which stage are you on right now, and which one do you want to play out your life on in the future? What do you need to do to get to that stage? Return to the letter that you wrote earlier and edit it if needed to reflect any new goals.

Pick a role that you currently have and imagine the stage expanding. What would the role look like on a grander stage? What would you need to do to stretch to a larger platform?

What are the hurdles on the road to your objective? Which ones are external and which are internal?

# Unlocking Motivation

What really motivates you? Consider the short term, the intermediate term, and the long term. Think about that question in regard to different aspects of your life, including family, education, work, and community.

Fill out the Passion–Confidence matrix with activities in your life that fit into the four quadrants. Ask friends, family, or colleagues to do the same, and share your results. Discuss why you placed specific items in each quadrant and whether there are ways to move some of the items into the upper-right quadrant.

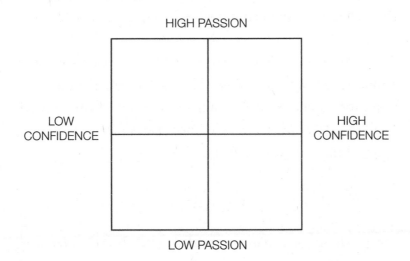

HIGH PASSION

LOW CONFIDENCE        HIGH CONFIDENCE

LOW PASSION

# Experimenting

Practice making pretotypes. Pick a few challenges/opportunities in your life—big or small—and design and perform different types of pretotypes to evaluate the feasibility of various solutions. Consider what approach you will use for each—the Mechanical Turk, the Pinocchio Technique, or the Fake Door. For example, how might you create a pretotype for a new item on a restaurant menu, a pillow with a built-in alarm clock, or an app that offers personalized exercise protocols?

Look at the list of things that motivate you from the prior chapter and design some experiments that would address these challenges/opportunities.

Do an experiment; try something you've never done before and see what happens! It can be a social, physical, or intellectual experiment. Actively evaluate the results of the experiment to extract what you've learned. Does this motivate you to do additional experiments in this area?

# Focusing

See how long you can focus on a project without interrupting yourself. Pick a quiet spot and a task that you want to accomplish. If you find yourself easily distracted, look for ways to eliminate them, one by one. For example, close your computer, shut off your cell phone, and remove from your desk items that draw your attention.

What's in your trash compactor? What things might you delegate or eliminate?

Review the matrix designed by Greg McKeown on page 117. Are you not only focused on the right things, but also able to actively focus? If not, what do you need to do to get into the upper-right quadrant?

# Reframing

Practice homuncular flexibility by learning to write or brush your teeth with your nondominant hand.

Pick something in your everyday life that you don't enjoy, and find ways to make it enjoyable. Think of ways that you could look at the situation differently and specific things you could do to change the experience.

Look back at the goals you have set for yourself and come up with a list of crazy ways you could accomplish them. Figure out how you might make those ideas work in reality.

# Persisting

Make a list of all the resources you have. Start with the obvious things and then dig down to identify other tangible and intangible resources available to you.

Take a few "steps" this week that are a bit larger than you think you can handle. For example, volunteer to do something that will take more effort than you usually expend, or tackle a problem that looks complicated at first glance. Afterward, spend some time on reflection. Were the results as you expected, or were you able to handle the larger step gracefully?

How high is your "ocean"? How far below the surface are the mountains? Can you identify the specific mountains that are closest to the surface? What are you doing to stay replenished? What more *could* you do?

# Inspiring Others

Tell or write your life story three times. The first time, focus on all the terrible things that have happened to you. The second time, focus on all the wonderful opportunities you've had. And the third time, tell your story as a comedian would, focusing on the funny episodes.

Use the story spine framework to tell several stories. Practice presenting these stories to your friends, family, and/or colleagues.

Consider your own presence, warmth, and power. Which of these characteristics do you exhibit, and which could be enhanced? Pay attention to those around you and privately notice their presence, warmth, and power. How do these traits affect you and others?

## Reviewing Attitudes and Actions

Return to the letter you wrote about your goals for yourself. Edit the letter again. This time include all the attitudes and actions that are required at each stage of the Invention Cycle.

Having gone through this process, make a list of your key insights. What did you already know and what is new? How will what you've learned influence your attitudes and actions going forward?

# Insights

_____

_____

_____

_____

_____

_____

_____

_____

# Acknowledgments

Every book has a story that begins long before you read the opening words. This book started its life in the spring of 2013, when I got itchy to write another book. I'm driven to write because the process demands me to design a lens through which I'll look at the world for the next year or so, and forces me to organize my experiences and my thoughts, leading to valuable insights.

Each book is an entrepreneurial endeavor. It begins with acute observation in order to identify a meaningful problem to solve, followed by the process of envisioning the ways I might address it. For this book, I tackled the challenge of developing a clear pathway through the entrepreneurial process, enabling anyone to craft the life they dream to lead.

Directing my attention mobilized my motivation. I began experimenting with different ways to capture the entrepreneurial journey, crafting a range of potential frameworks and drafting dozens of tables of contents, until I found a model and approach that fit. The first ideas were incremental, but

Acknowledgments

they became progressively more interesting as I connected ideas and gathered feedback from others.

A breakthrough finally occurred when I was able to look at the problem with a fresh perspective. This involved zooming out to see the challenge in a larger context. From there, with gathering momentum, it took many more months to accumulate relevant case studies and research that will, hopefully, inspire others to embrace the ideas.

Although I do all of my writing during long stretches of silence, the process is far from solitary. I draw upon input and inspiration from a vast number of people. It's my pleasure to recognize those who've contributed to this effort.

I appreciate all those who talked with me as I was developing the ideas for this book, sharing their experiences and providing feedback. This includes Steve Blank, Bill Burnett, Rich Cox, Tim Draper, Anna Eshoo, Dave Evans, Anne Fletcher, John Hennessy, Debby Hopkins, Marie Johnson, Sal Khan, Kai Kight, Ann Muira Ko, Julia Landauer, Kevin Meirer, Beverly Parenti, Lewis Pugh, Chris Redlitz, Heidi Roizen, Kate Rosenbluth, Justin Rosenstein, Mike Rothenberg, Alberto Savoia, Elad Segev, Piya Sorcar, Michael Tubbs, Tristan Walker, Don Wettrick, and Kay Young. I also mined STVP's extensive archive of lectures for insights from the speakers in our Entrepreneurial Thought Leaders lecture series, including Olivia Fox Cabane, Scott Harrison, Ben Horowitz, Guy Kawasaki, and Justin Rosenstein.

In addition, thanks go to all those who read the manuscript and provided meaningful feedback, including Deanna

Badizadegan, Joachim Bendix Lyon, Jason Cheng, Justin Ferrell, Steven Greitzer, Hussain Kader, Fern Mandelbaum, Heidi Roizen, and Yael Wulfovich.

I want to thank my colleagues at Stanford University. They couldn't have been more supportive. This includes Jennifer Aaker, Jeremy Bailensen, Steve Barley, Steve Blank, Leticia Britos Cavagnaro, Tom Byers, Ben Colman, Rich Cox, Dimitre Dimitrov, Persis Drell, Rebecca Edwards, Chuck Eesley, Kathy Eisenhardt, Justin Ferrell, Margot Gerritsen, Nancy Harrison, Matt Harvey, Aleta Hayes, Peter Glynn, Riitta Katila, Sarah Khan, Dan Klein, Tom Kosnik, Fern Mandelbaum, John Mitchell, Laurie Moore, Michael Pena, Jim Plummer, Heidi Roizen, Bernie Roth, Amin Saberi, Anais Saint-Jude, Nikkie Salgado, Eli Shell, Danielle Steussy, Bob Sutton, and Jennifer Widom. Special thanks go to the department of Management Science and Engineering, the Stanford Technology Ventures Program, and the Hasso Plattner Institute of Design at Stanford. Each day I'm fortunate to learn from my talented colleagues and students.

All of the work at the Stanford Technology Ventures Program is dependent upon support from generous donors who are enthusiastic about teaching young people to do more than imaginable with less than seems possible. Big thanks to Jim Breyer and Ping Li at Accel Partners; Tim Draper, Steve Jurvetson, and John Fisher at Draper Fisher Jurevetson; Debby Hopkins and Debbie Brackeen at Citi Ventures; Gordy Davidson, Dan Dorosin, and Mark Leahy at Fenwick and West; Tina and Trygve Mikkelsen; Aubrey Chernick;

and all the STVP alumni who continue to support our programs.

This project never would have come to life if it hadn't been for my spectacular colleagues at HarperOne. Gideon Weil is the best editor in the universe. He provided me with just the right dose of pressure, the perfect level of guidance, and endless encouragement. I looked forward to every conversation with Gideon as he helped me shape and polish this book. I also appreciate all those at HarperOne who contributed to the project, including Claudia Boutote, Kim Dayman, Hilary Lawson, Terri Leonard, Adrian Morgan, Kathy Reigstad, Renee Senogles, and Lisa Zuniga. Special thanks go to Mark Tauber, HarperOne publisher, who welcomed me into the HarperCollins family many years ago.

Finally, I am indebted to my wonderful family and friends for their encouragement, including my parents, my son Josh, and his wife Katie. A huge shout-out goes to my remarkable husband, Michael. For the past thirty years, he has provided unfaltering support, crucial feedback, thoughtful insights, and unending love even through the darkest times. There is no way I could have completed this book without him on my team. Michael, I love you. You are my superhero.

# References

## Letter to Readers

Tina Seelig, *What I Wish I Knew When I Was 20* (San Francisco: HarperOne, 2009).

Tina Seelig, *inGenius: A Crash Course on Creativity* (San Francisco: HarperOne, 2012).

Stanford Technology Ventures Program website, http://stvp.stanford.edu.

## Introduction

The Last Mile website, https://thelastmile.org.

For more on the nine-dot puzzle, http://en.wikipedia.org/wiki/Thinking_outside_the_box.

Jim Adams, *Conceptual Blockbusting,* 4th ed. (New York: Basic Books, 2001).

Mark A. Runco and Garrett J. Jaeger, "The Stanford Definition of Creativity," *Creativity Research Journal* 24, no. 11 (2012): 92–96.

Sir Ken Robinson, "Can Creativity Be Taught?," http://youtube/vlBpDggX3iE.

Biodesign Innovation Fellowship website, http://biodesign.stanford.edu.

## Part 1: Imagination

Scott Harrison, "Thirsting for a Life of Service," Stanford lecture, Nov. 6, 2013. You can find video clips of this speaker at Stanford at http://ecorner.stanford.edu.

Charity:water website, http://www.charitywater.org.

# References

## Chapter 1: Engage

Jennifer L. Roberts, "The Power of Patience," *Harvard Magazine* (online), Nov./Dec. 2013, http://harvardmagazine.com/2013/11/the-power-of-patience.

Nicholas Carlson, "Lyft, a Year-Old Startup That Helps Strangers Share Car Rides, Just Raised $60 Million from Andreessen Horowitz and Others," May 23, 2013, http://www.businessinsider.com/lyft-a-startup-that-helps-strangers-share-car-rides-just-raised-60-million-from-andreessen-horowitz-2013-5.

Chip Conley, *Emotional Equations* (New York: Atria Books, 2013).

Scott Barry Kaufman, "From Evaluation to Inspiration," Aug. 27, 2014, https://medium.com/aspen-ideas/from-evaluation-to-inspiration-26636af27c62.

Dave Evans and Bill Burnett, "Designing Your Life," *Stanford Open Office Hours,* Jan. 30, 2014, http://youtube/YKEq5iEmMSo.

## Chapter 2: Envision

Julia Landauer's website, http://www.julialandauer.com.

Angie LeVan, "Seeing Is Believing: The Power of Visualization, *Psychology Today* (online), original post written Dec. 3, 2009, https://www.psychologytoday.com/blog/flourish/200912/seeing-is-believing-the-power-visualization.

Kevin Meier, Flint Books, http://www.flintbooks.me.

Elad Segev, "When There Is a Correct Answer: Exercise in Creative Thinking," May 9, 2013, http://youtu.be/9TskeE43Q1M.

Caroline Bologna, "Letter from LEGO to Parents in the '70s Makes an Important Point About Gender, Nov. 24, 2014, http://www.huffingtonpost.com/2014/11/24/lego-letter-from-the-70s_n_6212362.html.

"Jeff Bezos," no date, http://www.biography.com/people/jeff-bezos-9542209.

Martin Luther King, Jr., "I Have a Dream," address delivered Aug. 28, 1963, http://www.americanrhetoric.com/speeches/mlkihaveadream.htm.

Kai Kight, "Composing Your World," TEDx talk (Manhattan Beach), Dec. 4, 2014, http://youtu.be/eGGhlLW3GUA.

Steven Levy, "Google's Larry Page on Why Moonshots Matter," *Wired* (online), Jan. 7, 2013, http://www.wired.com/2013/01/ff-qa-larry-page.

Miguel Helft, "Larry Page: The Most Ambitious CEO in the Universe," *Fortune* (online), Nov. 13, 2014, http://fortune.com/2014/11/13/googles-larry-page-the-most-ambitious-ceo-in-the-universe.

Felipe Santos and Kathleen Eisenhardt, "Organizational Boundaries and Theories of Organization," *Organization Science* 16, no. 5 (2005): 491–508.

Karol V. Menzie (on Nancy's Quiches), "Entrepreneur Carves Out Niche for Quiche in 'Real' Food Market," *Baltimore Sun* (online), Oct. 13, 1993, http://articles.baltimoresun.com/1993-10-13/features/1993286028_1_make-quiche-make-quiche-mini-quiches.

Ann Miura-Ko, "Founding Thunder Lizard Entrepreneurs," Stanford lecture, Oct. 27, 2010. You can find video clips of this speaker at Stanford at http://ecorner.stanford.edu.

Michael Tubbs, TEDx talk (Stanford), May 11, 2013, https://tedx.stanford.edu/2013/michael-tubbs.

Heather Barry Kappes and Gabriele Oettingen, "Positive Fantasies About Idealized Futures Sap Energy," *Journal of Experimental Social Psychology* 47 (2011): 719–729.

Olivia Fox Cabane (on the impostor syndrome), "Build Your Personal Charisma," Stanford lecture, Oct. 10, 2012. You can find video clips of this speaker at Stanford at http://ecorner.stanford.edu.

## Part 2: Creativity

On the New York City Opera, http://topics.nytimes.com/top/reference/timestopics/organizations/n/new_york_city_opera/index.html.

Craig Duff, "Finding Tomorrow's Classical Fans," *New York Times* (online), May 24, 2014, www.nytimes.com/video/arts/music/100000002900637/finding-tomorrow8217s-classical-fans.html.

Melena Ryzik, "The Entire Audience Dozed Off? Perfect!," *New York Times* (online), May 16, 2014, http://www.nytimes.com/2014/05/17/arts/dream-of-the-red-chamber-and-other-sleep-oriented-shows.html.

*Sleep No More* (immersive theater experience) website, http://sleepnomorenyc.com.

## Chapter 3: Motivate

Don Wettrick, *Pure Genius: Building a Culture of Innovation and Taking 20% Time to the Next Level* (San Diego: Dave Burgess Consulting, 2014).

# References

Daniel Pink, "The Puzzle of Motivation," July 2009, TED talk (global), http://www.ted.com/talks/dan_pink_on_motivation.

Daniel Pink, *Drive: The Surprising Truth About What Motivates Us* (New York: Riverhead Books, 2011).

Amy Wrzesniewski and Barry Schwartz, "The Secret of Effective Motivation," *New York Times* (online), July 4, 2014, http://www.nytimes.com/2014/07/06/opinion/sunday/the-secret-of-effective-motivation.html.

Mayfield Fellows Program website, http://stvp.stanford.edu/mayfield-fellows-program.

Guy Kawasaki, "Make Meaning in Your Company," Stanford lecture, Oct. 20, 2004. You can find video clips of this speaker at Stanford at http://ecorner.stanford.edu.

John Gardner, "Personal Renewal," address delivered to McKinsey & Company, Phoenix, Nov. 10, 1990, http://www.pbs.org/johngardner/sections/writings_speech_1.html.

Khalida Brohi (panelist), "Mobilizing for Impact," Clinton Global Initiative, Oct. 2013, http://youtu.be/8i0EatUx088.

## Chapter 4: Experiment

Michelle Trudeau, "Preschoolers Outsmart College Students in Figuring Out Gadgets," NPR, June 30, 2014, http://www.npr.org/blogs/health/2014/06/30/325230618/preschoolers-outsmart-college-students-in-figuring-out-gadgets.

For Alberto Savoia on prototyping, see http://www.pretotyping.org.

Peter Sims, *Little Bets* (New York: Random House Business Books, 2011).

Rich Cox's website, http://peoplerocket.com.

TeachAIDS website, http://teachaids.org.

## Part 3: Innovation

Katherine Young's website, http://www.kbyoung.com.

## Chapter 5: Focus

Olga Khazan, "Precrastination: Worse Than Procrastination?," *Atlantic* (online), Sept. 24, 2014, http://www.theatlantic.com/health/archive/2014/09/precrastination-worse-than-procrastination/380646.

# References

Epicenter Innovation Tournament website, http://epicenter.stanford.edu/
resource/innovation-tournament.

Justin Rosenstein, "Leading Big Visions from the Heart," Stanford lecture,
May 8, 2013. You can find video clips of this speaker at Stanford at
http://ecorner.stanford.edu.

Tristan Harris, "Distracted? Let's Make Technology That Helps Us Spend
Our Time Well," TEDx talk (Brussels), Dec. 16, 2014, https://www
.youtube.com/watch?v=jT5rRh9AZf4.

"Mindfulness in the Age of Complexity," *Harvard Business Review*
(online), Mar. 2014, https://hbr.org/2014/03/mindfulness-in-the-age
-of-complexity.

Cliff Nass, "Are You Multitasking Your Life Away?," TEDx talk (Stanford),
June 20, 2013, http://youtu.be/PriSFBu5CLs.

Daniel Levitin, *The Organized Mind: Thinking Straight in the Age of
Information Overload* (New York: Dutton, 2014).

Greg McKeown, *Essentialism: The Disciplined Pursuit of Less* (New York:
Crown Business, 2014).

Stephen Covey, *Seven Habits of Highly Successful People,* anniversary ed.
(New York: Simon & Schuster, 2013).

Dave Ulacia (on Covey's principles), "Are You Working on the Wrong
Things?," Apr. 28, 2009, http://getorganized.fcorgp.com/content/
are-you-working-wrong-things.

Diane M. Beck and Sabine Kastner, "Top-Down and Bottom-Up
Mechanisms in Biasing Competition in the Human Brain," *Vision
Research* 49, no. 10 (June 2, 2009): 1154–1165, in-press version used,
https://www.princeton.edu/~napl/pdf/BeckKastner2008.pdf.

William D. S. Killgore, "Effects of Sleep Deprivation on Cognition,"
*Progress in Brain Research* 185 (Jan. 2010): 105–29.

## Chapter 6: Reframe

Mauricio Estrella, "How a Password Changed My Life," May 14, 2014,
https://medium.com/@manicho/how-a-password-changed-my-life-
7af5d5f28038.

Ian Urbina, "The Secret Life of Passwords," *New York Times* (online),
Nov. 23, 2014, http://www.nytimes.com/2014/11/19/magazine/the-secret-
life-of-passwords.html.

Alina Simone, "The Spread of Mondegreens Should Have Ended with
the Internet, but It Hasn't," PRI, Nov. 20, 2014, http://www.pri.org/

stories/2014-11-20/spread-mondegreens-should-have-ended-internet-it-hasnt.

Department of Defense, Crisis Communication Strategies, "Case Study: The Johnson & Johnson Tylenol Crisis," no date, http://www.ou.edu/deptcomm/dodjcc/groups/02C2/Johnson%20&%20Johnson.htm.

Douglas Heaven, "Learn to Shake Your New Tail as a Virtual Animal," *New Scientist* (online), June 20, 2013, http://www.newscientist.com/article/dn23725-learn-to-shake-your-new-tail-as-a-virtual-animal.html#.VOoElsb3_Yo.

Jaron Lanier, "On the Threshold of the Avatar Era," *Wall Street Journal* (online), Oct. 23, 2010, http://www.wsj.com/news/articles/SB10001424052702303738504575568410584865010.

Tristan Walker, "Be an Authentic Entrepreneur," Stanford lecture, Apr. 9, 2014. You can find video clips of this speaker at Stanford at http://ecorner.stanford.edu.

Rosamund Stone Zander and Ben Zander, *The Art of Possibility* (Boston, MA: Harvard Business School Press, 2000).

## Part 4: Entrepreneurship

Mike Peña, "Experiential Learning Essential to Entrepreneurship Education at Stanford," Sept. 26, 2013, http://stvp.stanford.edu/experiential-learning-essential-to-entrepreneurship-education-at-stanford.

## Chapter 7: Persist

Lewis Pugh, "How I Swam the North Pole," TED talk (global), Sept. 2009, https://www.ted.com/talks/lewis_pugh_swims_the_north_pole.

Duckworth Lab (University of Pennsylvania) website, https://sites.sas.upenn.edu/duckworth/pages/research.

"The Entrepreneur Failures Behind the Success of Richard Branson," Mar. 14, 2014, http://www.nextupasia.com/the-entrepreneur-failures-behind-the-success-of-richard-branson.

Gregory Warner, "Fleeing War and Finding Work," NPR, Aug. 15, 2014, http://www.npr.org/blogs/money/2014/08/15/340421054/fleeing-war-and-finding-work.

# References

## Chapter 8: Inspire

Liz Wiseman and Greg McKeown, "Managing Yourself: Bringing Out the Best in Your People," *Harvard Business Review* (online), May 2020, https://hbr.org/2010/05/managing-yourself-bringing-out-the-best-in-your-people.

Ben Horowitz, *The Hard Thing About Hard Things* (New York: Harper Business, 2014).

Chip Heath and Dan Heath, *Made to Stick* (New York: Random House, 2007).

David Eagleman, *Sum* (New York: Vintage, 2010).

David Aaker, "Skype Uses Storytelling to Drive Growth," Dec. 17, 2014, https://www.linkedin.com/pulse/how-skype-used-storytelling-david-aaker.

"Kurt Vonnegut on the Shapes of Stories," Oct. 4, 2013, http://youtube/9-84vuR1f9o.

Maya Eilam, "The Shapes of Stories: A Kurt Vonnegut Infographic," Jan. 1, 2012, http://mayaeilam.com/2012/01/01/the-shapes-of-stories-a-kurt-vonnegut-infographic.

Teresa Norton, "Story Spine: A Simple Exercise to Get You Unstuck," July 25, 2012, https://hbr.org/2012/07/a-simple-exercise-to-help-you.

Kenn Adams, "Back to the Story Spine," June 5, 2013, http://www.aerogrammestudio.com/2013/06/05/back-to-the-story-spine.

"This Advice from IDEO's Nicole Kahn Will Transform the Way You Give Presentations," no date, http://shar.es/1W5yiV.

Bob Sutton, "Scaling Up Excellence," Stanford lecture, Feb. 12, 2014. You can find video clips of this speaker at Stanford at http://ecorner.stanford.edu.

Robert Cialdini, *Influence: The Psychology of Persuasion* (New York: Harper Business, 2006).

Olivia Fox Cabane, *The Charisma Myth: How Anyone Can Master the Art and Science of Personal Magnetism* (New York: Portfolio/Penguin, 2013).

Olivia Fox Cabane, "Build Your Personal Charisma," Stanford lecture, Oct. 10, 2012. You can find video clips of this speaker at Stanford at http://ecorner.stanford.edu.

## Conclusion

Tim Brown, "Design Thinking," *Harvard Business Review* (online), June 2008, https://hbr.org/2008/06/design-thinking.

Steve Blank, "Why the Lean Startup Changes Everything," *Harvard Business Review* (online), May 2013, https://hbr.org/2013/05/why-the-lean-start-up-changes-everything.

Steve Blank, "How to Think Like an Entrepreneur: The Inventure Cycle," Sept. 9, 2014, http://steveblank.com/2014/09/09/how-to-think-like-an-entrepreneur-the-inventure-cycle.

Ben Keene, "Schools for Life," Oct. 15, 2014, https://medium.com/@benkeene/schools-for-life-eadd9b85ceee.

Draper University website, http://draperuniversity.com.

# Index

# Index